The Girls with the Grandmother Faces

Not *"How-to"* but *"Why Not?"* for Today's
Most Interesting New Breed of Women

by
Frances Weaver

PRICE STERN SLOAN
Los Angeles

Copyright 1987 by Frances Weaver
Published by Midlife Musings
P.O. Box 970, Saratoga Springs, New York 12866

Distributed by Price Stern Sloan, Inc.
11150 Olympic Boulevard, Suite 650, Los Angeles, California 90064
Printed in the USA
10 9 8 7 6 5 4 3 2

ISBN: 0-8431-2900-X

FOREWORD

Frances A. Weaver first came into my view ten years ago like Mary Poppins, swinging on a kite string. Her letter to Vogue about the Beulah Valley Association for Tethered Flight (a bunch of non-young women flying their kites in the Colorado mountains) tipped me off to qualities she still displays--originality and independence. In fact, I'd use two of her own words to describe her: *decisive, self-propelled.* Her new book is stuffed with sound, usable advice for the widowed ("single and sixty") woman; in fact, as one who was widowed at forty-two, I can tell you that her ideas work for any age.

I was struck by Frances's clear-eyed comments in this book on the subject of happiness. I think she would endorse a quotation that has proved helpful to me over twenty years; it's from Edith Wharton's novel *The Last Asset:*

> "There are lots of ways of being miserable, but there's only one way of being comfortable, and that is to stop running round after happiness. If you make up your mind not to be happy there's no reason why you shouldn't have a fairly good time."

Following the wise Weaver instructions could lead to a fairly good time that will feel a lot like happiness.

—Lorraine Davis
New York City, 1987

CONTENTS

Foreword 3

Introduction 6

Widowhood--A Different Kind of Single

Chapter One 9
Good Housekeeping Seal of Approval

Chapter Two 13
It's My Turn Now

Chapter Three 17
Thirty-four Years to Grow On

Chapter Four 21
The Launching of Fran Weaver

Chapter Five 25
How Old Is Old?

Family Life--The Team Without the Coach

Chapter Six 29
Revolving Doors, A New Family Life

Chapter Seven 36
Oma and Her Big Ideas

Friends--A Whole New Ball Game

Chapter Eight 40
A World Filled With Old Women

Chapter Nine 45
Who Needs a Ride to the Party?

Chapter Ten 50
New Contacts, New Skills

Moving Is a Lot Like Making Love

    Chapter Eleven 56
      Our Place or Mine?

    Chapter Twelve 59
      Me and My Shadow

The Men In Our Lives--Where?

    Chapter Thirteen 61
      Just Ask Me to Dance--Please

    Chapter Fourteen 65
      Wilt Thou Take This...

Travel: When? Where? How?

    Chapter Fifteen 68
      Hearts: Young--Hair: Gray

    Chapter Sixteen 72
      Get Set--GO!

    Chapter Seventeen 78
      Of Slow Boats and Taking Notes

    Chapter Eighteen 83
      Amtrak; the Road Back

Support Groups

    Chapter Nineteen 87
      Join the Crowd!

Your World Is Waiting--Don't Miss It

    Chapter Twenty 91
      Twenty Percent Still to Go

ADDENDUM: Back to the Classroom 95

    Elderhostel and Writing Courses

INTRODUCTION

Not many years ago I was in the middle of a busy morning. Sarah was tagging along, helping me around the house.

"What're you doin', Grandma?"

"I'm straightening the living room. The girls are coming for bridge this afternoon."

"What girls, Grandma?" By now the kid was jumping on the couch.

"You know, Sarah. The girls I play bridge with on Wednesdays. My friends...."

"Yeah, yeah. I know!" she crowed. "You mean the girls with the grandmother faces."

Those girls are my peer group, my generation. We constitute the fastest growing segment of our population. Women over 55 have more discretionary buying power, better health, better housing, more freedom to move around, more opportunities for continuing education, more leisure time, more labor-saving devices, more knowledge of the world around us than any single group in the history of the world. Ever. We also have 20 percent of our lives still ahead of us with choices available for improving the quality of our lives as never before. We are, in a very real sense, blessed by the world in which we live.

It is to these women, the girls with the grandmother faces, this book is primarily addressed. Why? Why would a kite-crazy housewife from Beulah, Colorado, ("a little mining town in the West") feel compelled to write a book pointing out the advantages of being old? Why doesn't this dingbat woman take life easy, lunch at the Club, work on the church bazaars, rest on the laurels of her surgeon/hero husband or look for a new husband instead of leaving her family 2,000 miles behind, starting college all over and launching a new career just when the rest of us are ready to throw in the towel?

When I was turning 40 I watched the 60-year-old women I knew best including my mother. I had first envied these women because they had all of the advantages I was waiting for: grown children with established families of their own, leisure time every time day since they no longer cooked for a family, kept house for five or six messy kids, ran errands from dawn to dusk from the orthodontist to the Y, or had mud-stained jeans or football uniforms to contend with. Those women have time to do all of the things I wish I could do now, I thought.

Then I took a closer look. Listened to what those older women were saying. I heard nothing but complaints:

"Life is such a bore now the kids are grown. I have nothing to do. And they never call home except for money."

"TV is just terrible. Except for 'Jeopardy' and 'Days of Our Lives' there's nothing to watch."

"I'd like to take a trip but we have to go where George can play golf. Which I don't do, of course."

"Cooking for the two of us is stupid."

"I guess Jack's wife is a nice enough girl, but they never have time for me. You'd think after John died...."

"Here we have this wonderful place in Palm Springs and the children refuse to come out here to see us, even for Christmas."

For Pete's sake, I wanted to yell at them, you have all the time and the freedom in the world. What about all those gripes you had about never having time for yourself?

Avoiding those pitfalls of boredom and stagnation became a crusade with me. No way would I let myself get into a rut or lose my enthusiasm for the world around us. Too much is at stake--the rest of our lives.

So this book is addressed to the women my age, widowed or married, who are intrigued by the possibility of changing lifestyles to take advantage of opportunities. For the risk-takers of our world I offer suggestions, to those fearful of making decisions I offer encouragement. (Look at the middle of that word.) To those of you who want to make more of your lives in this important period I offer hope.

Most important to all of us is attitude. The sincere desire to lead a productive, interesting life at any age depends upon our own imagination and acceptance of new ideas. How do you know you can't operate a word processor? How do you know you can't go back to the classroom? How do you know there's no room for you in the "outside world?" What makes you so sure you cannot play a guitar or speak Spanish or paint a landscape? What convinces you that you can't travel on your own? Drive across the country with your grandkids?

The best resource any of us have is ourselves. I have used my own experience as primary research for this book. To my adventures as a runaway grandmother/kiteflier/student/writer/traveler I have added expert advice from wise friends and family members including my mother who is much younger now than she was 20 years ago. I have also read and quoted from authorities on aging.

This book has been fun for me to write. I hope it's a joy for you to read.

CHAPTER 1
Good Housekeeping Seal of Approval

What was it like--that little girl world we lived in more than 50 years ago? How did we picture ourselves as grownups? What was important? What did we do? What did we expect?

By the time I was old enough to go to school, I assumed I would one day be an old lady like my grandmother. It was my intention to be exactly like her, but if Grandmother Allison and I could stand side-by-side today, the only similarity would be our weight. She was a hefty, well-corseted woman. So am I.

Growing up in Kansas, my sisters and I needed only to cross the street to go to Grandmother's. She lived in the old Victorian where my father and his six sisters had been raised. I sat on the same front porch, ate at the same table, played in the same attic, slept on the same sleeping porch, explored the same fruit cellar, swung under the same tree and swiped the same soft ginger cookies my dad had thrived on. My cousins--some from as far away as Illinois or California--adored Grandmother and her cookies, too; but I believed the proprietary rights were mine.

My grandmother was always at home. Except for church circle or meetings of the library board, I cannot recall her going anyplace. Before Grandfather died she had traveled with him. There were stereoptican views and album photos of Yellowstone Park and Santa Monica, and page after page of pictures of the family on vacation in Colorado--perched on huge boulders--wearing long skirts and wide hats. But Grandmother stayed at home when I knew her. Her groceries were delivered, her doctor made house calls, she did not own or drive a car.

9

Family gatherings were rituals. Norman Rockwell would have had a field day when the clan swarmed in with assorted cousins accompanied by *their* cousins from the surrounding countryside. Middle America straight from the cover of the *Saturday Evening Post*. I pictured myself in that same setting, being that kind of a grandmother in that kind of a family.

Now here's the most important recollection about my grandmother which I wanted to emulate the most: she never yelled. I do not think of her as a controlling woman, but we never felt obliged to misbehave to test her. When we ran in the house or quarreled about trifles, she would say, "Hark, hark." Nothing more. To me she epitomized a woman totally comfortable with her surroundings, her place in the world. Old age was apparently exactly what she expected it to be. Unruffled, she sat on her porch or in the "middle room". She taught us to crochet. She read heavy leather-bound books and recited long poems by heart. I knew I'd be just like her--some day.

Fifty years ago that block where Grandmother lived was populated by single women, all of whom looked old to me. Richard Armour claims, "There's nothing new about old age." In this case he's right; old women have outnumbered old men for a long time. The last man to live on the block in my memory was Grandmother's bachelor brother, Uncle Bill, but he didn't last nearly as long as the old girls did. Next door, with her widowed mother, was Daddy's and my first grade teacher, Miss McDonald. Next to them lived Miss Anna Bukey, then came our (Dad's and mine) sixth grade teacher, Miss McElvain, with her mother. Next neighbor was Mrs. Guymon, and so on. We knew all of these women well, mostly because of their front porches. We skated, jumped rope, and raced on bicycles past their houses. They were the old ladies who bought our first Girl Scout cookies.

What kept these women in their homes? Their homes did, I've decided. Before household chores evolved into a few minutes of button-pushing, these women had something to do all day long, as much or as little as they wanted. Take the laundry, for example: On Monday morning every woman on that block (often with her hired girl) collected everything in the house and dragged it down steep narrow steps to the basement. They shoved the brutishly heavy Maytag over next to the tubs and started running water. They would run water all day long. Piles of clothes, table and bed linens and towels were sorted all over the floor, which became wet as the day wore on. After the machine was filled with the hottest water, the entire house reeked with the fumes of Fels Naphtha, Rinso, or 'P and G'. Grandmother kept a wooden spoon to break up lumps in the soap. Then she'd fill tubs with rinse water and start the wringer routine. Every item went through that wringer three times. Some went round and round and had to be pulled out, others were bulky enough to pop open the rollers. Water dripped in every direction no matter how carefully the wringer was positioned. (The basement floor stayed wet until at least Thursday, so the basement smelled damp forever.) All morning long, wet-heavy baskets of sodden towels and sheets were hoisted up the steps to the clothes lines. Grandmother or Esther--her right hand--spent at least two hours every Monday in the back yard with a mouthful of clothespins, wrestling with wet sheets. Then another two hours in the afternoon, retrieving the clean clothes and linens. This was the day's activity. It needed to be done, they were needed to do it.

To do my laundry, I don't even have to be at home. The same is true of the other household chores. I can cook without being there. Cleaning and ironing are miniscule tasks compared to the heavy housework of Grandmother's generation.

This, to me, is the primary reason my life at 60 is--can be--different than the life I pictured for myself by observing my grandmother.

So what else is new in the last 50 years? Personal contacts, to start with. The fabric of American life began to disintegrate with the disappearance of the front porch. This is my own observation; don't expect to find it in any learned psychology book. When we moved to the patio in the backyard, then to the TV in the house, we lost important human contacts. Evenings were a time of sociability up and down Grandmother's block. The older folks sat on their porches while the younger ones stopped by to visit. Lemonade was found on every front stoop in those days. Sometimes we could sit on the porch and listen to the band concert over in the park. Other nights we went to the park to hear the music and eat popcorn and catch lightning bugs while our parents chatted with their friends sitting in the cars. But we were together with our neighbors.

"My mother always had someone to talk to," my wise friend Michael says. "The vegetable man, the clothes man, the laundry man, the milkman, the guy who sold linens--the Jewel-T man--she talked to all of them. Now she has maybe the checkout girl at the supermarket and her doctor. Nowadays my mother's doctor is supposed to be a listener for all of her complaints--and she's mad at him most of the time because he hasn't time to hear all she wants to say. She needs someone else to talk to as she had when we were growing up. I'll never forget the day the man came to our block selling four-way-stretch girdles. That was the biggest day of the year. All the women followed him down the street, watching how long he stayed at every house. My

11

mother misses that." Michael's mother is no different than most of the oldsters I know.

The world I expected to be old in was shaken to its core in the '40's, started to fall apart in the '50's, and nearly capitulated in the '60's; resulting in total transformation by the '70's. My impression of old women from my childish, impressionable years was no longer valid, or even logical. With automated housekeeping and acceptance of women in the work force (beginning with Rosie the Riveter) women's attention turned to wider social issues, thence to establishing their own identities. Establishing her identity never occurred to my grandmother. She knew who she was.

Mother's generation, women now in their 80s, patterned their 60s after their mothers, even though times had changed so dramatically. Being 60 meant being at home on the shelf. Favorite sayings were, "A woman my age should never..." or "I'm too old for...." or "My mother always said..." I don't believe they realized they had at least 20 years ahead to spend--some way.

Being 60 certainly doesn't mean being at home on the shelf anymore. The message is clear; we cannot live like our grandmothers did--nor our mothers. Women who do not maintain an active interest in the world around them are of no interest to anyone else. Failure to expand our own horizons is certain to lead to an old age of loneliness and boredom. It is our own fault if we allow that to happen. The most important asset in a woman's life is probably flexibility.

That's a fact, Ladies. The world has changed, and so must we in spite of our childhood dreams of being like Grandma.

CHAPTER 2
It's My Turn Now

"It's just that I'm so lonely. Like last weekend I went to our cottage at the shore. My son and his family said they'd join me there, but on Saturday morning the phone rang and I knew without answering that they had something to do in town and I'd be at the beach alone--where we used to have so many good times. I could hardly stand it."

Five minutes before she said this, this woman and I had been total strangers in a crowd of strangers. She was trim, well-dressed, articulate, but her mouth was pulled down at the corners in self-pity. I know that gal, I thought. She's one of us--the girls with the grandmother faces.

The others sitting at the luncheon table with us smiled sympathetically. "We know how hard it is," said the women next to her. "Adjusting to being a widow sometimes takes a lot of time. Coming along on this trip to Oxford with this Smithsonian crowd is a good start for you."

Mercifully, we were not subjected at that moment to another recitation of the woes of widowhood. In my circle these days, that is often the most popular subject next to aging--which is equally painful for some women.

Later on, after I decided I really liked this little lady from Virginia, I had a chance for a private conversation. "How long ago did your husband die?" She was appalled that I would use that terrible word. There seems to be an unwritten law among the conspicuously grieving that "die" is never said right out loud. She expected to be asked, "How long have you been alone?" or, "When did your dear husband pass away?" That's the liturgy of widowhood among older women. They heard someone, sometime, say, "Never say die," and took it literally.

That oblique language is also a means of hiding from the truth. Dying is a fact of life. (The people who tickle me the most are those who say, "If I die." What other plans do they have in mind?) Facing death and the way it completely changes the lives of the survivors is also a fact of life. My new friend needed to know that.

She went back to the subject of the beach cottage and her loneliness. "Maybe you don't need that cottage any more. Maybe it no longer fits into your life. Have you considered selling it, or renting it-- that could be nice extra income." She didn't give me time to go into my discourse about the tax advantages of income properties which is just as well; I don't actually know that much about such things. Instead, she stared as though I had suggested she remove her right arm.

"But we've had that place at the shore for 20 years. How could I sell it? Allow strangers to move in there with my things--Herb's things! He'd have a fit."

"It's not Herb's problem anymore. Herb died. You didn't. It's your turn to make the decisions. It's your turn, now, to live your life the way you want to. You have yourself to answer to. If you are miserable with some arrangements of your life, DO something to change them. Nobody else will. You've had months to figure that out-- not just the beach house, but expecting your son and his family to keep you company. You're a grownup. Single for the first time in your life. These can honestly be good years. Don't miss out by wallowing in what used to be. Appreciate your life for what it has been and what it can be. You learned a lot about living that you don't even know you know. Surprise yourself. Take charge. Nobody is trying to say your life will be better without your husband, but it will have to be different. That's only common sense." She finally smiled and we walked on to Worcester College for another class.

Believe me, I don't go around with my soapbox delivering this tirade to every woman I meet--just the ones I think can take it. There are a lot of them.

More than half of the women over 65 in America are widows. Older women are also the fastest growing segment of our population. In terms of absolute numbers, that means there are literally millions of women who no longer have husbands.

So why do so many of the widows I meet act as if this "catastrophe" had never happened to anyone but themselves? Why do some of the brighter ladies have such a tough time accepting their new role in life? That's for the psychologists to answer, certainly, but my own deduction is that loss of married life takes away a safety net. We

14

have used our husbands and our families as a shield, a buffer, an excuse for not making our own decisions or recognizing our own capabilities. Younger women have gotten into this "self-fulfillment" business. We who are in our 60s have not made that commitment to ourselves until we are suddenly on our own. We have to play catch-up.

For years I have been acquainted with a woman who has devoted the past 12 or 15 years of her life to being a full-time widow. You know the kind--the weepers you dodge between the aisles in the supermarket to avoid meeting. Everyone in town knew her husband. He was a nice guy; had many friends. To hear her tell it, you'd think she was married to a cross between Abraham Lincoln and Francis of Assisi. When this cry baby traps anyone between the cereal and the dog food shelves, the ritual of sanctification is repeated. Pictures are dragged from her wallet. The cornered listener stands nodding helplessly while the ice cream softens and the minutes tick away. Finally she goes on her way carefully composing the remorseful look on her otherwise pleasant face. She pulls the same stunt with bank tellers, clerks, and the man at the dry cleaners. Why? Because she has never put forth the energy or imagination to make a life of her own. She has no real regard for herself. That's very sad.

Another old friend is more direct about her dependence on her husband. Jean had been president of the medical auxiliary. She had two daughters of whom she could be proud. She was active in her church and community affairs. When her husband died after several heart attacks, vascular surgery and other such important warning signs that her life was about to change, Jean repeated again and again, "I never was anything but a doctor's wife. Now I'm not even that!"

Now she's lonely and bored. Maybe some day soon she'll change her outlook--start looking out instead of in.

Widowhood is a rite of passage in the strongest sense of the words. Our lives have changed and can never be the same again. The friends, the social life, the financial priorities, our relationships with our children, daily routines and leisure time, the way we eat and the way we sleep are all new. It's almost like starting over.

"This woman is too critical of widows. She must have been a terrible wife or had a lousy marriage," you are saying to yourself about now. Maybe so, but certainly no woman in her right mind wants her husband to die. Neither would she want him to go on living in pain--an invalid--for her own convenience. The human body is a fragile, mortal piece of equipment. We are fools to expect too much of it. Grieving has its place, but it is for the living, not the dead, that most of us

15

grieve. ("I need him so!") The real danger is in adopting grieving as a way of life. That's a cop-out because you're still making your husband responsible for your own well-being: hanging your life around his neck.

My husband was a man of great compulsions. His work and his patients were intensely important to him. For him to have survived the attack which killed him, he probably would have been a cardiac cripple, if not an invalid, for the rest of his life. I wouldn't wish that on my worst enemy, let alone the father of my children--the man with whom I had shared good times and bad times for 34 years. I could not make him young again in perfect health. Nobody could. That's not facing reality.

John Weaver was also a man of monumental faith. At the risk of sounding preachy, so am I. The basic secret of successful living, widowed or not, is serenity to accept the things we cannot change. One of the women I have admired for years made the remark after the death of her 80-year-old husband: "Well, I guess I'll just have to accept the fact that he isn't here anymore." What ELSE was she going to do? Where are the choices?

The rest of the Serenity Prayer applies particularly well to the shock of finding oneself adrift and alone after losing a spouse (as they say). Courage to change the things I can. Remember my friend with the beach cottage? And wisdom to know the difference. That's the toughest part.

CHAPTER 3
Thirty-four Years to Grow On

It's necessary to tell my own story here to qualify what I have to say on this subject.

There's nothing startling to tell. My husband was just getting out of the army, starting to medical school when we were married. The first ten years of our married life were centered on his education and his career. I had a bachelor's degree in medical technology, but my secret plans of becoming important in his professional life vanished with the first baby--eleven months after we were married. After that, my biggest job was keeping the children quiet so Daddy could study, or filling in as both parents when internship, residency, and combat duty in Korea interfered with family life. Our third child, Ross, was born while John was on active duty in Korea; John never saw him until Ross was a year old. That was okay. We could take a lot in those days. We had one common goal: general surgery.

Understandably, my husband's practice remained the paramount part of our lives even after the training days were over. I never was one of those old-fashioned women who referred to her husband as "doctor." As a matter of fact, however, there were times when I was convinced I needed to present my Blue Cross card to get his attention. The kids and I lived around him, in a way. I busied myself with civic affairs, politics, the Episcopal ladies, and the Colonial Dames, but the basic decisions, the nitty-gritty of our lifestyle and activities, were governed by John, just as his father had done in the household where he grew up. I was, in effect, a dutiful wife who knew her place--not without resentment--on days ending in 'y', as John used to say.

"As John says...." or now, "As John used to say...." has been a part of my conversation for years. John was a wise and witty man with his own way of expressing his thoughts. His imprint on our family is unmistakable.

17

We spent a lot of time laughing at our house. Jokes came easily to all of us, not simply story-telling, but spontaneously funny reactions to ordinary situations. When John was asked by one of his colleagues if he was making plans for retirement, John fairly bellowed, "Hell, no. How many times a week can anyone clean the ******** garage?"

In the operating room one day John announced to the assembled nurses, technicians and others, "My wife and I were having a little game in the living room last night and we discovered a new position." Stunned silence and astonished stares greeted this statement until he explained, "We found out you can put the dominoes back in the box either sideways or lengthwise."

One old patient felt better on the day she said, "Doctor, tell me the truth. I'm going to die. Right?"

He took her hand and replied, "Yes you are, Mrs. Curry, and so am I. But I don't think either one of us will do it today."

Our prize byword for the holidays came from John: "It's Christmas, Goddamit! Be pleasant!" I can still see him in the midst of torn Christmas wrappings, crying kids and spilled hot chocolate at dawn, wondering how Christmas had turned into such bedlam--again-- and it wasn't even daylight yet.

Compassionate was a good word for that husband of mine though he often remarked when family affairs required sympathy and understanding, "I gave at the office." His own description of himself was, "I'm a humanitarian sonofabitch." And he was.

In the late '60's, John ("Dr. Christian") felt so strongly about the spread of communism and the war in Vietman, he took time off from his practice twice in two years, two months at a time, to serve as a volunteer surgeon in civilian hospitals in Vietnam. On the Mekong Delta he cared for the people of Phu Vinh and was there during the in-famous Tet Offensive of 1968.

The people of Pueblo decided they had a local hero when John wrote home asking for supplies for a Vietnamese orphanage. Everyone in town collected diapers, bottles, lotion, clothes, vitamins and toys to be sent for his distribution. One group even collected old bowling shirts for the refugees. (I have a great picture of a tiny Vietnamese man engulfed in a red shirt reading "Pueblo Brake and Clutch.") The patients and hospital personnel there appreciated their big American doctor. He was called "Bac Si Beau Coups Kilo," which translates to "Doctor of many pounds." Back home after these tours of duty with the AMA-sponsored program, John gave speeches and showed slides of the great improvements in sanitation and hospital facilities because of American medical involvement.

He was a born leader and a basically good man. His family lived in his reflected glory.

Death ended our marriage abruptly. John went up to bed before I did one evening seven years ago. When I went upstairs an hour later, he was dead--no pain, no disability. He would never have to face retirement or perpetual garage-cleaning or other ways to spend leisure time he did not enjoy. He'd never worry about younger surgeons spoiling his magnificent practice. He was 55. So was I.

Two years before this happened, I had started to write for magazines, mostly by accident. This was the one project I had taken on which had my husband's absolute approval. He read much more than I did, and was delighted to discover I was literate. It also pleased him that I stayed at home to do this. When my first article about flying kites appeared in *Vogue* magazine, John bragged to his colleagues about it. He had been forced to buy only a typewriter for me. His partner had bought his wife a gift shop.

On the day I started to think of myself as a writer, John came home at noon on a Saturday to find me weeping in the kitchen, clutching a letter, really sobbing.

"NOW what?!"

I showed him the letter, written in the wiggly script of an old woman. "I loved your article in *Vogue* about Beulah, Colorado. It brought back many memories of my college days and my friend...who might be dead by now...."

"A stranger," I blubbered, "an absolute stranger telling me about her friend in Beulah. And I found the old friend and she's not dead, and she's going to write to this lady."

"Fine. Fine. But why are you so torn up about all this?"

"Because I touched somebody. Because something I wrote has touched a total stranger. Because now I'm a writer. Now I'm a writer."

I don't think he really understood--how could he? Surgeons touch people all the time. At least he didn't make fun of my crying, and that was nice.

Believing halfheartedly in "signs" has always been a part of my life. Soon after John's death, writing seemed to me to have come into my life in preparation for widowhood. I felt the same way about the purchase we had made of a small house across the road from our home in Beulah, Colorado. That was certainly the signal for me to move.

19

During the first year I floundered; made a lot of mistakes. In the first place, I expected my married children, single son, and grandchildren to be ever-watchful and available for their widowed mother. When it became obvious they were not going to drive 30 miles from Pueblo to spend Sunday afternoons with me, I told myself it was understandable with their own family plans. But I roamed around the house and yard feeling very sorry for myself. It never occurred to me--at first--to call my widowed friends. I wanted my offspring there in spite of my constant protestations that I could cope with life on my own.

I bought a small condominium in Pueblo--nearer to family and friends. This was primarily a social move. Couples, two or three at a time, were invited for cocktails at my adorable little pad. I thought they had left me off their guest lists because I'd have a long drive home by myself. The grandchildren and my daughters-in-law would drop by after school, I fantasized. In other words, I wanted to make myself the center of everyone's lives although I would have knocked anyone out of the ballpark for suggesting this as my motive.

The ploy did not work. I paced the floor like a caged mother bear in that condo, waiting for the world I had known so recently to beat a path to my door. No way. I had to turn the corner completely--realize my life would have to change entirely--before I settled down to a satisfying lifestyle of my own making. Writing, travel, and college courses made it happen.

CHAPTER 4
The Launching of Fran Weaver

In this country today among people over 65, fully 80 percent of the men are married, more than half of the women of their age group are widowed and most of us live alone. Only one old man in eight lives alone. Accepting these truths as gospel, immutable fact did not come easy. I had never been an active feminist, but the double standard for the over-the-hill gang upset me for a while.

During these first months of widowhood I truly resented widowers--those men who were invited to every party and never were expected to repay the invitations--those men who could walk confidently into any restaurant and expect a decent table--those men who could ask any woman on the cruise for a dance and walk away--those men who were socially in demand at all times, in all places. Yet they turned their attentions to younger women and the women my age sat at home because a single man is a plus at any party, but a single woman probably needs a ride home. Now I know this is a fact of life, as surely as the sun sets in the west or Lake George freezes in January.

At the end of my first floundering year I was convinced that physical separation from home for a while--a real change of scene--might be helpful. Except for a couple of writers' conferences and visits to a relative or two, I had never traveled by myself. "Well, Frances," I announced to myself one day, "it's time for you to find out how grownup you really are." And I booked a 30-day cruise.

"Are you going ALONE?" My buddy Martha was flabbergasted. "Yep," I said bravely, wondering what I should be frightened about. That first outing gave me the answer: nothing. There are nice people to meet and new friends to make all over the world. I had only to reach out to others on my own to find a sense of honest identity. Being in a crowd of strangers is bewildering, but my reward far outweighed the initial feeling of being alone. On that ship I met fellow passengers who would know me only for myself. I was nobody's wife, or mother, or daughter, or committee chairman, or Den Mother. I was just me. It was up to me to prove myself worth knowing. I had dropped the safety net. It felt good.

Traveling on that cruise ship felt so good, in fact, I wanted to share the experience with other women and older couples. How? During my career as the world's greatest generic chairperson (You find a cause, I'll get a committee) I had served as chairman for fund-raising trips sponsored by the Colonial Dames. I knew how to organize travelers as a volunteer. Why not go through the same motions as a semi-professional?

I called my travel agent friend, Judy Smith, to announce she had a new employee: me. I also informed her that I would organize and sell group tours for her agency if she would provide expertise on reservations, computers, and do the bookkeeping. My cut was to be 20 percent of her gross commission. I was responsible for promotion and travel details. Fine.

I literally launched myself as a tour director with a big party at the Pueblo, Colorado, Country Club. Three cruises had been arranged for 1982. First, a Trans Canal cruise in February. Second, a European port cities cruise in May. Third, a cruise of the Inside Passage to Alaska in August. Writing letters, sending out clever brochures of my own creation, making hundreds of phone calls and personal interviews, I sold sufficient passage on the February and August cruises on Royal Viking Lines to qualify for an agent's rate. Most of my customers were friends, or friends of friends. We had a generally good time. I had found a way to travel at reduced rates and make travel easier for women fearful of going places on their own. I was growing.

The next big step came when I was raving to my youngest son about Adirondack Community College, where I had been one of the panelists for a writers' workshop. My subject had been Starting to Write After 40. Again I was standing only on my own two feet. Matthew listened to my carrying-on about the campus, the school, the people and finally said, "Don't you hear yourself, Mother? You're not telling ME to go to that school. You're saying YOU should go to that school." Bless him.

Two thousand miles is a long way away to go to college, but I did it. Right after I returned from the Alaska cruise I headed east. My grandaughter Sarah and I started school the same day; she went to kindergarten, I went to college. Her grades are better than mine, but we have each had a great time.

The send-off for my new college career was a magnificent display of family support. First of all, my mother in her 80's was encouraging about my going off to school. My daughter in Houston was enthusiastic. But it was my sons and their interest in my renewed academic endeavor which impressed me most. As a farewell gesture I had treated the family to an Italian restaurant the night before my departure. Chris--number one son--insisted on coffee at his house afterward.

Once in Chris and Mary's living room I found myself seated in the big chair, surrounded by children and grandchildren. They want to wish me a pleasant journey and hope I have a good time, I thought. No way. There followed a lecture about the advantages and responsibilities of college life. The same speech each of them had heard from their father and me when they had gone off to school:

"Now don't think you're going to college just to have a good time with your friends."

"Take courses that will be a challenge for you, Mom. Don't stick to the easy stuff. You're not really dumb, you know."

"You'd better have a budget. No need to spend a lot of money on fancy restaurants or more clothes. Your stuff is good enough. Besides, you're already laying out out-of-state tuition."

I was cautioned about getting into too many extracurricular activities too soon, so I promised not to run for homecoming queen 'til the fall of '83. They stopped short of warning me about unwanted pregnancy.

They did approve of my leasing my Pueblo condominium during my absence. That showed some fiscal responsibility, I suppose, but their skepticism about my ability to handle money surfaced with their attitude about my use of credit cards. Only for emergencies. I decided they'd heard too much from their father about my spending habits.

Midsummer of '82 I had stopped off in the Glens Falls area long enough to find a place to live for my budding new life as a student. Two rooms at the Nassau Motel on Lake George Road would suffice. The back room was a large bedroom; the front room was everything else. The kitchen was corner cupboards, refrigerator, sink, and stove top--no oven. A dinette set and four chairs plus a hide-a-bed couch completed the furnishings. The place was new, clean, and efficient except for the miniscule closet.

Two of my sisters agreed to drive east with me in my big move, another supportive effort which I appreciated. We took ten days to mosey across America, stopping along the way to see everything from the arch at St Louis to Gettysburg and Harpers Ferry. We ate hot fudge sundaes at Hershey and rode the Circle Line Cruise around Manhattan Island. When we arrived in the Adirondacks, they thoroughly approved of my living arrangements, which made me feel even better.

Not since John's freshman year in medical school had I lived in such quarters. This added to the sense of adventure--a new beginning. I bought a wok and eventually a word processor which crowded the place considerably, but I loved the new freedom from "things". The living room was barely big enough to seat six people, but I gave supper parties for my new friends and had a marvelous time.

Late in the spring, after seven months at the motel, I found a condominium for rent at Cannon Point on Lake George; necessary because of an impending visit from my mother. One bedroom, one bath and no view of the lake was all right for a freshmen like me, but hardly suitable for houseguests. That condominium sealed the deal between Upstate New York and me. I had found my second home "fitting" in every sense of the word.

Now I live part-time in the Adirondacks and part-time in Colorado. In the east I am only me, although I've insisted each of my children and their spouses visit Lake George to check it out. It's important to understand each other's motives in the family. They approve. That helps. There will be plenty of time when they might have a helpless old woman on their hands, needing care. In a way, we're all taking turns, for a few years, anyway.

CHAPTER 5
How Old IS Old?

"Fifty is a time of final options, but it is also a culmination, the prime of life, the beginning of seeing how it all turns out. Let there be less marveling at our wonderful preservation and more respect for the maturity of our mind and spirit. After all, the most important mission of a woman's life is not to hold onto her looks. Our mission is the same as a man's...to grow up. To ignore that goal is to exclude women from adult responsibility. Fifty is 50, and to deny that is to deny wisdom, experience and life itself."

These were the words of Jane O'Reilly in the *New York Times* on July 10, 1986. She also said: "This third of my life is for me. These are my final options." Well, Jane is a mere child of 50, but her opinions make even more sense at 60.

Which brings us to the second subject: aging. Volumes and tomes have been written about aging. It's a popular subject for scientific study and amateur speculation. More and more of us are living longer and longer so the subject is inexhaustible. The census charts concerning aging are astonishing. We oldsters are the fastest growing segment of the population. If we weren't so tired we could take over the whole world.

Some writers are more astute about aging than others, of course. One of the best, to my mind, is M.F.K. Fisher whose book, *Sister Age*, represents the accumulation of observations and opinions about aging which Ms. Fisher has been collecting for a lifetime. She writes, "The Aging Process is a part of most of our lives, and it remains one we try to ignore until it seems to pounce upon us. We evade all its signals." How true. We recognize the fact that we live this long because we have not succumbed to smallpox, tuberculosis, or typhoid fever as we would probably have done in the past century. We also know that nutrition, sanitation and sterilization have produced healthier oldsters than have been known in past generations. But we are reluctant to say, "I'm old." When a tactless (I could say mean, or cruel) houseguest said to me, "Are you ONLY 60?" I felt like belting her in her dentures.

The focus on youth on television and in every other aspect of our culture makes us almost ashamed to admit how old we are. A Beverly Hills woman I met not long ago was bragging about the one last favor she performed for her 90-year-old mother when she died. "I had the mortician cut five years off her age on her tombstone." Now really.

But we are all living to riper old ages. I have three sisters and an 86-year-old mother. When my mother was starting to complain about some minor detail of our lives, I told her not to worry; in just a few years all of her children will be on Medicare. That's too true to be funny. It also illustrates the fact that a 60-year-old woman has at least 20 years to go, so she'd better stay alert and healthy. Someday MY kids will be this old.

My heroine, M.F.K. Fisher, continues: "What is important, though, is that our dispassionate acceptance of attrition be matched by a full use of everything that has happened in all the long wonderful-ghastly years to free a person's mind from his body...to use the experience...so that physical annoyances are surmountable in an alert and even mirthful appreciation of life itself."

The key word is "alert." One of the most memorable travel experiences I have had was the Smithsonian/Oxford Seminar because of the ages of the participants. Of the more than 100 Americans living and studying at Worcester College, Oxford, more than half were at least 60. That's an unscientific estimate based on my own observations. There were many widows, a few single men, and a number of couples. Students of traditional college age were conspicuously absent. Students under 40 were rare.

What were all those old people doing--eating sloppy English oatmeal and cold toast for breakfast in a medieval dining hall which resounded to the point of making most conversation impossible? What did they hope to accomplish by hoisting themselves out of ordinary dormitory beds to charge off to some classroom to hear lectures about literature, Renaissance art, prehistoric Britain, or the archeology of Oxfordshire? They were keeping their curiosity alive--their heads turned on. Some were reviewing old facts, others were on their first trip to England and wanted a responsible overview of the country. Basically, these men and women were enriching their own lives, thereby remaining in the main stream. In furthering their own interests, they would be of interest to others. When those oldsters talked about the "good old days" they probably meant 1066 A.D.

The shelves of every local library are loaded with books about the negative side of aging. Chronic diseases, financial planning, grief--all are covered by more authoritative sources than I could even pretend to be. The positive side of aging is what we are studying here. I agree with Richard Armour when he comments: "I hope I have a young outlook. Since I have an old everything else, this is my one chance of having a bit of youth as a part of me."

Having a young outlook is vastly different from looking young. On the shelves of any bookstore or library, during the commercials in any soap opera, in the pages of any magazine, we can all learn how to look young--or so the claims go. Looking young seems to be Priority Number One of Everywoman's World. I have never figured out exactly why. It would seem to me that any woman who likes herself at all, likes herself at any age.

Although I cannot tell you how to take 20 years off your thighs, I can give you my never-fail rules for looking OLDER:

1. Wear the same bright red lipstick that looked so good on you in the '40's.
2. Use enough dead-black hair color to give the impression you've been shampooing with Dyanshine.
3. Talk about your diet, your bad back, your teeth, your son-in-law and your bladder at every opportunity.

The never-fail rule for feeling better about being older is maintaining a sense of humor. One charming grande dame in Colorado Springs claims she copes with her failing memory by feeling her toothbrush before she brushes her teeth. If it's wet, of course, she knows she's already done that. What a young outlook she has! And what a joy she is to be around.

CHAPTER 6
Revolving Doors--Family Life

"It's okay with me if you want to move to New York, Mother. You don't need my permission, for God's sake. Just answer one question for me, though. Are you moving *from* something or *to* something? 'Cause if you're going two thousand miles to get away from the rest of us, we all have a problem."

That was number two son, Ross, after I announced my intention of enrolling in Adirondack Community College for the fall semester of 1982. His concern was appreciated and exceedingly well stated, I thought. He was almost wrong in saying I didn't need his permission, however. The subtle reversal of roles between my children and me had begun on the night of their father's death, although we did not recognize the fact until much later. For a while we kept running into each other, getting in one another's way, in the revolving door between our old family structure and the new one we were all seeking.

These same convolutions occur with any change in family numbers--divorce, new marriages, more children. The trick is to come out of such upheavals with an improved working relationship among the survivors. Dependence has to be redefined. Exceptions are modified. Family life cannot go on in the same old way any more than any other drama once the cast of characters changes.

I certainly did not need permission to go east to college. What I did need was their approval--for my own peace of mind. The children became the review board for the parent. Women my age have made few, if any, major decisions on their own. Our parents expected obedience and acceptance of their plans for our lives. We consented without much fuss. Then our husbands took over the decision-making process in our traditional families. After all, they were the breadwinners. We expected to be second in command. Some of us have a really hard time trusting the momentous decisions we must make now we are on our own. We can learn. That's a top priority project.

Family life needs a re-balancing for these later years. It's similar to changing strategies on the playing field. Somebody else is "it". That's an unfamiliar position for a mother from the '40's and '50's to play without the coach sending in new signals from the sidelines. I know where I want the game to go, but I was unsure, at first, of my ability to call my own plays. It took practice, time, a few mistakes, and a lot of understanding. That adds up to a new maturity of which I am mighty proud.

"Just leave Ross and Judy (or any of our offspring) alone about this," I used to yell at John. "They're adults. They deserve the chance to make their own decisions and live with their own mistakes." Looking back, I'm certain I sounded that tolerant and understanding when I agreed with what the younger generation Weavers had in mind. I felt I had to get Good Old Dad off their backs, but I knew if matters really became traumatic, Good Old Dad would rescue all of us. Eventually, they came around to their father for the advice they needed. Nobody is reminding me to keep my nose out of the internal affairs of four Weaver households. I must do that myself. Every day. They are solid citizens--that family of mine--yet for some reason the urge to direct their lives seems even stronger now that I am a single parent.

Look at it this way: When John was alive, we had some heated discussions about our children and their growing-up problems. But we talked them over with each other more than we tried to argue with the youngsters involved. We aired our feelings about their crises with each other. Now I cannot do that, but I still have the urge to "talk things over", so I find myself bringing up subjects with my sons, daughter, and rarely with their spouses which are absolutely none of my business. I just want to hear myself expound my great wisdom. That's bad.

My mother has the same problem. My mother is an active, alert woman of 86 who has devoted every minute, every thought of her adult life to her four daughters. She is first, last, and always a mother. We are, and always will be, her children. She has no real idea how old I am. My birth date is engraved on her memory, yet she still fusses about the shoes I wear, the cars I drive, the company I keep. Whenever I am about to appear in public to read from my work or make some sort of speech, she is a nervous wreck. She's my mother.

I have reminded her of my advanced age--it seems to me we should be equals in the judgment department by this time--and we find ourselves more and more in agreement these days. Sometimes, as a matter of fact, I'm convinced she's getting younger while I'm getting older.

My feeble joke about all of her children being eligible for Medicare was not at all funny to my mother. I wonder why. Easy; Mother knows kids my age cannot even understand Medicare.

My sister is moving into an elegant townhouse. Mother worried about her finding new friends in the neighborhood. "I don't know any young people who live there." When I suggested my sister might ask around for a local chapter of AARP, Mother was not amused. Neither was my sister. So I suggested PTA. Worse.

This longevity business creates more four-generation families than ever before in our history. Perhaps some of us stay more alert and active in our 60s because we're still trying to prove to our mothers we can think for ourselves--which is what we are also trying to prove to our own children.

I'll tell you this much: Whenever I feel I've been neglected by my own children or grandchildren, I rush to the phone to call my mother. Maybe I should ask her for advice more often. She'd love that.

What do I have the most of right now? Time. My time is my own to spend as I see fit. How can I best share this precious commodity with the most important people in my life--my family--without taking too much of *their* time; without going into my Girl Scout leader routine or laying on some sort of "After all, I AM your mother," guilt trip and running everyone's lives?

I heard a marvelous description of the pitfalls of this latter day Family Planning during a writers' workshop at the Smithsonian: "My mother serves up guilt on a platter--with the turkey at the family Thanksgiving dinner." Quite a lesson there. We want to spend time with our families, to be available when needed, without intruding on their own family life--just as we hoped our own parents would do.

Forget the guilt part--the sense of obligation. If you and I have done so much for our children because they happen to be our children, we don't have to remind them how wonderful we are or how much they owe us. The pleasure we had being involved in the shaping of their lives is an adequate return. Whatever fun we have with them now is an unearned bonus. This can be the best time we've had with our own kids if we have sense enough to consider their feelings whenever some big idea hatches in our heads.

In his book, *60 Plus*, Allan Fromme, psychologist, advises people with grown children to fill our lives so full of things to do and people to see we have no time for parenting. He's right, you know. We have so many opportunities and advantages around us, we have no business expecting our families to provide recreation and entertainment for senior citizens. I have expanded Fromme's succinct advice into some reminders of my own.

First, the DON'TS:

DO NOT: Drop in unannounced.

Insist upon family gatherings for all holidays.

Ask the same questions more than once a week.

Expect constant displays of gratitude.

Try to "buy" excess consideration.

Plan outings without consultation.

Offer advice unless specifically asked.

Insist upon paying all the dinner checks, or
refuse to pay your share of the dinner checks.

Reminisce over and over again.

Contradict or interrupt habitually.

Turn down invitations, waiting for the family to call.

Say, "Your father always said...."

or, "My father always said...." That's worse.

This is a partial list. It boils down to being ourselves with an active life of our own instead of draping ourselves around our family's necks like some heavy old-fashioned cameo to be cherished only for past glories, real or imagined. Never forget, nothing makes any of us seem older than conversation and activities centered on the good old days.

Here are the positive suggestions for Oma Weaver's Helpful Homilies for Family Harmony:

DO: Make a concerted effort to find new topics of conversation with family members of all ages.

Concentrate on one-on-one experiences instead of group "command performances."

Be willing to travel to visit them instead of insisting everyone should "come home."

Reassure all family members of your availability and desire to help out in emergencies.

Demonstrate flexibility whenever you can.

Listen--listen--listen--listen--listen.

Plan outings with friends on Sunday afternoons.

Consult with parents before inviting some kid for a "treat" he might not enjoy.

Offer to run errands, help out, etc. only if both the spirit and the flesh are willing.

Stay alert for moments when the best thing you can do is disappear.

Add new interests to your own life without expecting family participation or enthusiasm.

Say "thank you" a lot.

Lest I sound too Goody-Two-Shoes for the reader, I hasten to add here that most of these do's and dont's have been learned the hard way. During the past six years I have gotten along very well with my sons and daughter and their spouses most of the time. It would be foolishness to claim we always see eye-to-eye, or agree about my plans for my life or theirs. One of the worst mistakes of my entire life was interfering with opinions and advice in difficulties between one son and his wife and their teenage boys. The pain I caused then was dreadful. It shall not happen again--a lesson not soon forgotten. Thank God for their tolerance of me during those days and their acceptance of me now.

One of our difficulties in dealing with the family problems of our children is the mistaken belief that such troubles are *our* problems at all. Also, we tend to look at the behavior of teenagers in an outmoded way, forgetting the world has changed while we were busy getting old, or trying to stay young. B.F. Skinner's marvelous book, *Enjoy Old Age*, cautions us strongly about using outmoded standards for today's youth. The same overworked ideas can get in the way of making a good time of leisure time with the family.

Consider the grandmother who lovingly planned a wonderful family outing to cut Christmas trees in the woods. "We always had such a great time doing this when you were little. Remember? We picked out just which tree looked best and decorated it while it smelled so fresh and piney. Won't your children just LOVE it? I'll bring the hot chocolate and the little sled. The one we always used. We'll leave really early on Saturday morning. Oh, Daddy would have loved this so!"

Saturday morning is bound to be a disaster, of course. One grandkid has a baseketball game. A teenage grandaughter has promised to go Christmas shopping with her friends. A perverse daughter-in-law cannot stand real trees because of the mess of needles on her new carpet. The dependable son calls to report trouble with the old reliable chain saw. And so it goes....

Two feet of old crusty snow cover the only remaining spot where cutting is allowed anymore. The parking lot is two miles downhill. None of the kids wear boots. Mittens are wet. Noses are running. The real hot chocolate is not as good as the instant stuff at home. The cookies have been broken and the trees closest to the road have been partially consumed by pine bark beetles. Three households have located only two decent trees. Suddenly it's time to rush home because The Game starts at one o'clock on TV.

The well-meaning grandmother drags her own wimpy little tree ("Oh, no, you take the fuller one. This is fine for me in my tiny place. I still have the ornaments you children made, so it'll be just fine for me...alone.") into her living room--and cries. Next week she'll complain to her bridge group about her ungrateful family who ruined the entire Christmas season for her.

That story reminds me of an old lady I knew years ago, back in Kansas. She said, "I don't care what they put on my gravestone as long as it doesn't say, 'She meant well.'" A sobering thought for our 60s.

One more point of sharing--as important as time to some of us--is money. The dilemma is relatively new. We have planned for our children to inherit our worldly goods when we die. If I live as long as the actuarial tables say I might, my children will be almost as old as I am now before they have the enjoyment or comfortable living that inheritance might provide. Allison, my pragmatic daughter, stated the case plainly, "We don't expect you to leave us anything, Mother, but we would appreciate it if you'd come out even."

Mine is probably a purely maternal attitude, one not gleaned from authorities on financial planning, but this is the pattern of my lifestyle right now. After making certain my medical care insurance is adequate and basic investments (mostly real estate and government mortgage whatevers) are secure for those coming days when I could be totally dependent on others, I will by George share all I want to with my youngsters now--while I can watch them enjoy it. And none of this making a scene about being fair. When my interest in this is equal, what I do for them will eventually come out even.

Several of the women I know feel this way. Others are still bound up in their belief that what was saved for our old age has to be sacrosanct until we die--and we have an obligation to reinvest any earnings in order to leave even more for our children. We have only to watch any of the soaps--starting with *Dallas*--to see what happens when families argue about money. Those shows are popular because every family faces these problems to some extent. We, the widowed mothers or the wives of retired fathers, can work out some of those problems before one of our kids drags the others into court if we keep an open mind about the importance of money.

What on earth is this woman talking about? The next chapter will spell out how I have put my financial sharing with the family into effect. So far, I've had no complaints.

But the most important sharing is time and attention.

Always.

CHAPTER 7
Oma and Her Big Ideas

"Dear Oma,

Thank you for inviting me!

I've been waiting to go to New York ever since I was an EMBRYO.

My mom says I will be there a week.

See you in Wa. D.C.

Love, S.J.W."

This letter from Sarah, written when she was eight years old, adorns the wall of my workroom--a constant reminder of the joys of grandmothering. I was in residence in the Adirondacks. Ross and his family would be vacationing in Washington. I asked to join them for two days, then bring Sarah home to visit me before we both returned to Colorado for the summer.

Since my big move to Lake George part-time, I have made sure every one of my family has a chance to inspect my home and lifestyle here in the east. It seemed important to me that they should be able to envision this life of mine away from them. Besides, I love this part of the country which has been unfamiliar to them and want to share. One or two at a time, all except the oldest grandson--now in the army-- have been here, including my mother and my sisters, of course. We have had some good times.

Intense planning has played a part here, particularly since the youngsters and I have a better time when we leave their parents at home. Flying to Albany is not that easy, so I have arranged to meet the kids in New York, then proceed together to Lake George. Here's how it worked once, in the spring of '84:

Two 13-year-old boys were involved. We carried out our rendezvous like the A-Team on assignment. I flew into LaGuardia from Albany at 10 o'clock. Whitney arrived from Houston at 11. Jason's flight from Colorado came in at noon. We ate lunch at the airport then took a 2 o'clock plane to Albany. My car was at the airport for the

36

drive to Lake George. For four days we played around in this area. Whit tried fishing but no luck. Otherwise we "messed around" and they played basketball with a smurf ball in my living room. Then we took Amtrak to New York City for two days.

There we did it all: the Circle Line Cruise, Empire State Building, a visit to the Stock Exchange, the Guinness Hall of Records, the Museum of Natural History, Hamburger Heaven, street vendors, *On Your Toes* and dinner at Mama Leone's. And more. Those boys still had enough energy to play smurf ball basketball in our hotel room. Then we did the airport routine in reverse. That's what I mean by spending some of the money which could be put away for their parents to inherit in 20 years or for these kids to have, perhaps, when they are in their 60s. Who wants to go to Hamburger Heaven or play smurf basketball at the Waldorf Astoria when he's 60?

My sons have been east for brief visits which made little sense to them, I suppose. They took time from their work for a weekend Upstate. Now they understand when I refer to places they've seen or talk about the condominium. Most misunderstanding can come within a family by not knowing a situation first hand. If they want to disapprove, at least they can be logical about it.

Family holidays are more relaxed than they were for a long time. We have had some memorable Thanksgiving dinners—memorable in a really negative way. Like the time one of my sister's kids brought two dogs along for the family gathering and it snowed so hard we were all trapped inside and our dogs didn't like her dogs. Or the time Chris dropped a root beer fizzie in the turkey gravy. Or some of the teenagers sampled the bar. Or the day when everyone invited seemed to have the impression I couldn't cook enough for such a crowd and showed up bearing bowls or pots of all sorts of stuff demanding space in the oven or the overloaded refrigerator. No more. Christmas is the same story. There used to be tension making all of the traditions work on Christmas Eve and Christmas Day. No more.

Christmastime in Beulah has been replaced by gathering in smaller groups wherever it's most convenient to get to church on time. The pomp and ceremony of ritual dining might work well in other families. We keep the whole affair simple, and enjoy each other and stray friends who drop by just as we are eating dinner.

Not all of our group projects or outings are expensive. Miss Sarah and I had a fine time last July in Beulah when she spent the night with me. We fixed our supper in the wok and the bamboo steamer, dressed up in what passed for kimonos, and sat on the floor eating our Japanese feast and drinking tea from little cups. She was kind enough to help me up when it was time to do the dishes.

Sarah and I have also enjoyed our miniature golf games and the Colorado State Fair. In Colorado Springs, various kids and I have toured everything from the museum of the American Numismatic Association to the Olympic Training Center. We have flown kites and waded in streams. We had ridden old horses at a dude ranch and spent hours in the Metropolitan Museum of Art. Nikki and I have driven cross-country from San Francisco, to Pueblo, Colorado. My sisters and I have found new fun being friends of old age when we drove from Colorado to New York together, sight-seeing all the way.

Outfits like the Smithsonian offer travel plans which are learning experiences for any age. Those same two boys who played smurf basketball at the Waldorf Astoria were with me in the summer of '86 for an archeological dig in southwest Colorado. Allison, my daughter, came along. We had a marvelous time in lectures and lab sessions, and the boys enjoyed the week as much as anyone in the crowd. Their fresh sense of humor was a tonic for the rest of us--all older folks.

Whitney and Jason entertained us by getting a spear caught in a tree outside the lodge with one mighty thrust of an atlatl, then heaving rocks at this huge cottonwood tree to dislodge the precious spear while the rest of us shouted encouragement. Whit did confuse one "tender-foot" nature lover by pointing out "rabbit berries" which he claimed came from "rabbit bushes". Oh well. Allison and I were proud of our two teenagers digging up more artifacts, sorting and cataloging them, than any other Smithsonian diggers. There are hundreds of other opportunities for intergenerational vacation experiences like this. We're already looking for the next one.

All of this is a different kind of togetherness than we had before I became a widow. John and I spent time traveling and vacationing, but I would be a fool to think I can do exactly what we enjoyed now that he isn't here. Not better, particularly, just different.

Two all-family excursions should be included here as suggestions for women uncertain about family travel. Once we went camping up near Aspen as we had done when they were children. My sons and daughter and their families. I was highly complimented to be invited and loved every minute. The boys had brought along a special tent and cot for me--all the comforts to be afforded an old lady. We ate trout fresh from the lake for breakfast, hiked and waded and had a grand time. That was special.

Then, instead of individual Christmas presents last year, I took those of the entire tribe who could get away to San Diego for a weekend. This was only possible because we are such a big family, the hotel gave us a group rate. That worked fine. We "broke up into smaller groups" for the most part--22 of us including my sister and her family. For this and for other outings in the future, the secret of success for all concerned is: don't suffocate each other. Some went to the zoo, some to Disneyland, some to see in-laws. We all went whale-watching on a three-masted schooner, but then again we did not cluster together like pigs at the trough. Each had his or her own fun.

Therein lies the secret of family activity when Grandma is the instigator. Give members of the group their own leisure time, their own space, as they say. I hope I don't forget that part.

CHAPTER 8
A World Filled with Old Women

Before you turn another page in this book I want you to stop for a minute--no more--and write the first five words that come into your head when you think, "Old woman." Right now. Jot the words here on the margin or on the flyleaf, or on the back of the nearest envelope next to that list you forgot to take to the market yesterday. Do not cheat by reading on. "Do not pass GO. Do not collect $200." Stop here and write five words, honest words. First impression words. What do you think of when someone says, "Old woman"?

I'll be fair about this. I'll reveal my list when I first confronted this challenge during a writers' conference two or three years ago. I wrote:

> bad breath
> poor posture
> lonely
> whining
> irritating

Others in the group added glowing adjectives like:

> boring
> repetitous
> self-centered
> old-fashioned
> poor

From that exercise I learned two instant lessons:
I have been an unreasonable snob about older women.
I do not want to be any of the above.
The wise woman conducting the seminar was not surprised by our answers. She then directed us to write five *positive* words about old

40

ladies. That took all of us a lot longer. My list was something like this:

> personal freedom
> leisure time
> chance to learn
> extra buying power
> good health

This is one of those workshop experiences which refuses to be packed away in the bottom drawer never to be seen again. These lists of five haunted me because they were about *me*. Only I could do anything about those negative and positive images. Nobody else. It had to be me.

The best way to attack any general problem is to reduce the question to specifics. When had I formed those negative images? Were they all from my childhood? Who were the old ladies with the bad breath and the poor posture? What older woman had been so irritating that I even thought of that word?

As a kid and as a young woman I was constantly aware of denture breath, coffee breath and smokers' breath. The principal reason I never smoked was the awful odor of smokers who insisted on whispering in my face. My parents' friends, aunts or older cousins would hug me and their breath was terrible. I resented the unpleasant aura around them almost as much as the inevitable remarks about how big I was for my age and the comments about how girls "...these days...." wear their dresses too short or "have no sense about comfortable shoes with good arch support."

The first individual to come to mind from my adult experience was a not-so-old woman on a small-ship cruise of the Scandinavian Waterways. She was a retired professional woman of some sort. Her complaints about the food, the crew, the itinerary were loud and incessant. Worse than that was her appearance. In six days, she did not comb her hair or change her dress. When the Swedish stewardesses offered to help her shower or clean herself up, she refused, saying, "I don't have to look at me. These other people do. I'll never see them again." She was surely right about that.

Then there was a standout passenger on another cruise who ordered fish for dinner on the second night out. Much to her surprise, since she had not asked about terms on the menu, the fish was covered with a hot Spanish-style sauce. One bite burned her mouth. The waiter hurriedly replaced the dinner, but that woman spent the rest of the cruise talking about her digestion and "the way they cook fish on this boat." To this day, if she's asked about her Alaskan cruise, her answer will not be a description of Russian dancers in Sitka or the museum in Juneau. You'll hear about that damnable fish sauce; if you're foolish enough to inquire at all.

On that same cruise was a dear lady, Mary Whelan. Mary should have posed for Norman Rockwell. Her smile is infectious, her laughter appealing. Anything which might have displeased her she treated as her own problem. Mary was a great favorite with our fellow passengers. Even though she was only 84 at the time--tiny, huggable, always wearing a sassy little hat of some sort--whenever anyone asked her age, she'd say matter-of-factly, "A Hundred." And that was that. The contrast between these two women was memorable, obviously.

There have been admirable older women in all of our lives. Recalling them and the particularly attractive characteristics seems to me to be a worthwhile exercise for shaping my next 20 years:

Mae Reed Porter lived in Kansas City when John was an intern and resident there. I saw her rarely, but each time was a real occasion for me. I'm certain she would never remember me at all from the few times we chatted during Pi Phi alumnae meetings. Mrs. Porter was tall, erect, not quite graceful. Her white hair was short, her face lined but pleasant. Mrs. Porter had traveled extensively by the time I knew her. In Baltimore, in the back room of a bookstore, Mae Reed Porter had found some early-day prints of a Scottish hunting party in the American West stuffed into a cereal box. Fascinated, Mrs. Porter set out in search of the identity of the hunters and the history of their expedition. From that cereal box beginning, she wound up writing *Across the Wide Missouri* with Bernard DeVoto. This great lady wore bright tartan capes. She was a presence wherever she was. Her mind was much quicker and more fertile than those of us less than half her age. Yet her travels and her writing were not necessary for her livelihood. Mrs. Porter could have joined the rest of her social set for lunch every Wednesday and cocktails regularly at the Mission Hills Country Club. Instead she was off to Greece or sequestered in some library finding out more about the world which so fascinated her--and vice versa.

Florence Means never wrote any widely-known books but she will always be one of my role models. Florence was also tall, an imposing figure of a woman in any setting. (Is this one reason I am so distressed about shrinking to 5'8" in my old age?) Florence's outlook never aged. She never shrank, at least in my eyes. She wore fine big hats and told funny stories about living on a sheep ranch or learning to fly a plane in her 60s. Nothing seemed to have happened in her world--near or far--that failed to interest Florence. Thinking back, that was her charm: she was always interested.

Lillian Morrison lived well into her 90s and her eyesight failed but she never lost her zest for living or her ability to keep up with the world around her. I was in charge of a group cruise--a fund-raiser--on board the Delta Queen in 1973. It worried me to have a 90-year-old passenger. On the first night out of Memphis when I spotted Lillian Morrison perched on a bar stool, wine glass in one hand, song sheet in the other, surrounded by younger people straining to hear what she had to say, I knew we were in business.

My own mother is remarkable at 86, even though she has a tendency to resist any sort of change, like wearing pantyhose or taking calcium. She does live alone, drive her own car, and manages her affairs far better than I do. The inevitable difference in my feelings about her in contrast to other old women is not unusual; I just wish she'd stop mothering me. If she could let up on being my mother, she'd be one of my best friends. In the past two years, since I have been writing about older women and we have been talking a lot about aging problems, my mother has become much broader in her outlook, more tolerant of younger generations--and she lives in the midst of three layers of family now. She's stopped aging, she's younger. For that I am grateful as a lesson in my own dealings with my grown children and their families.

These are wonderful women. Writing about them brings tears to my eyes. When I read this chapter aloud to my number three son, I started to cry over Mary Whelan, whom I still see regularly when I am in Colorado. This remembrance does more, however. It reinforces my determination to seek out the admirable, the worth-knowing older women in my world and make a conscious effort to be that kind of an oldster myself.

Friends of mine like Grace Callahan who heads up a writing group in Leisure World, Fran Bayless who never lets a small irritation like a broken hip get her down, Mavis Todd who swims every day and shares happily her expertise about foundations and grants and worthy causes.

Did you ever hear anyone say about an old woman, "She hasn't changed a bit in 50 years?" That's no compliment. Beware. Change is essential in every aspect of our lives, particularly in our social lives, which we need to consider here.

CHAPTER 9
Who Needs a Ride to the Party?

This chapter has had as many false starts as an 8-and-under swim meet. Only the chapter about sex gave me so much to re-think when I read the first draft aloud.

Today the problem of writing about our social lives as singles in our 60s is clear--and simple. I have come to the conclusion it's a matter of definition. According to the *The Concise Oxford Dictionary*, "sociable" means "ready and willing to converse, communicative, liking company, marked by friendliness, not stiff or formal." Therefore, "social" means "not fitted for or practicing solitary life, interdependent, cooperative."

Roget's Thesaurus suggests synonyms for "society": "friendship, companionship, intimacy, fellow-feeling, neighborliness, companionability, cordiality."

I asked my good friend Terry to describe her social life. She said, "Nil." Terry's been a widow almost as long as I have, five years or so. We are long-time friends. We've traveled together. She plays bridge every Monday with my sister. She plays golf most of the rest of the time. Terry is an attractive, bright, energetic, conservative lady. But she says her social life is nil. Terry's definition of "social" is "party". So was mine, until I really gave the matter some thought.

While looking up the words "social" and "society" in half-a-dozen reference books, I never once found the term "party" or "date."

Maybe our lives ought to be defined as "redefinition". During our entire lives we ought to re-evaluate what we do. Social life meant "party" for most of us for years but those parties changed as we aged. (It's important to use that word--aged. We have been aging since we were born. Aging did not suddenly invade our lives at 55.) Birthday parties and school Valentine parties were replaced by teenage parties in back yards, thence to college beerbusts out in the woods or dances at the sorority house. On to charity balls and the country club in our young-married phase, then we concentrated for years on at-home entertain-

45

ing for couples with a few widows thrown in as time went by. Now the time has come for another transition in our social thinking. It's just that simple.

B.F. Skinner in *Enjoy Old Age* puts it this way: "There is only one solution: escape from the control exercised by the fun you once had....Limit yourself to the kinds of things you enjoy *as you are now.*" I would change the word "limit" to "treat" in that quote because we are all capable of having a good time if we put forth just a little thought and effort. But the entertainment is different from past years and the effort must be our own.

This thought just came to me, illustrating what I'm saying: back in my college days we danced at a marvelous place, the Avalon Ballroom, which had a dance floor on springs. That's right; there were big springs under the wooden floor. When the place was filled, the whole ballroom bounced with the band. That was the greatest fun I could imagine at that time (although my sister claims it ruined my husband's dancing because ever afterward he just stood in one spot and bounced on *any* dance floor). If I were foolish enough to return to the Avalon Ballroom in downtown Aggieville in Manhattan, Kansas, today, I'd break a hip before the band finished "One O'Clock Jump." Times have changed and so have we, Girls.

Two old men met outside a supermarket in Florida. One was carrying a sack of groceries.

"What did you buy?"

"Oh, just some bread and cheese and a head of lettuce."

"Why'd you buy it all at once? You could have made three trips."

See? Even an errand to the market can be a social event--or three. Skinner, again, writes of an older woman who buys only enough groceries for one day; she forces herself to go out again tomorrow. More often than not, we'll see someone we know in the store; someone who might like to come over for a cup of coffee one day. Someone who might enjoy going to a band concert or a ride to the country to find some really fresh corn.

Walking is another social event, a chance to get out among 'em and maintain your health and your image at the same time. If the people who walk at 8:00 don't interest you, walk at 9:00 and so on. If one route is a bore, go another direction. Change. Being too tired or too lonely to get out of the house is not the reason to stay in; it's the result. Boredom is 99 percent self-inflicted. That's what this book is all about.

Spur of the moment entertainment is possible for us now that we don't have to be at home to put the roast in or start the potatoes, pick up kids here, deliver them there, be on hand (with a drop of O'Cedar behind each ear) when our lord and master walks through the kitchen door expecting a feast suitable for the Prodigal Son on any day ending in 'y'. We have our own time to make our own fun, to be "communicative, liking company."

Spur of the moment works. Next time you are standing at your kitchen sink, staring into space, feeling left out, ask one question: "What would I really like to be doing right now? Or tomorrow? Or this weekend?"

Unless your answer is, "Making love," with which I cannot help you, (see chapter 13) head straight for the phone. Do not wait 'til morning. Do not stop to analyze who asked whoever the last time. Call someone who is likely to be in the same frame of mind and suggest anything plausible--just to get out.

Or invite someone in. Right now. I do a lot of entertaining. By that I confess I'm entertaining ME as much as my guests. Some of my best little evenings have been launched by an extra piece of chicken. This is an age-change we can easily overlook. In pick-up excursions or last-minute get-togethers, I am entertaining myself and my friends. If they have a good time, swell. If I have a good time, that's even better.

This new slant, for most of us, on sociability whenever and wherever without written invitations or complicated arrangements wipes out the tendency to stick to the who-owes-whom pattern which has hamstrung so many older women. Exploring new territory, eating different food, studying the work of favorite artists (or unknowns), listening to readings in the local library or going off to a jazz festival or chamber-music-in-a-barn improves the quality of our lives. Expanding horizons and laying groundwork for new friendships and activities make life more interesting. Sulking in front of CBS News cannot do that.

Back to the title of this chapter, "Who Needs a Ride to the Party?" During my career as the greatest hostess west of any given point, I never failed to plan one big party during the summer when I invited all of our widowed friends. I'll bet you've done that, too. This was a ritual. The single women arrived together, generally sat together, and left together, but I was satisfied I had entertained the poor old souls. They were convinced my parties were better than eating corn flakes at home alone. I did not understand until widowhood engulfed me that those women would have had a much better evening one or two at a time in smaller groups. I expected them to appreciate sitting like birds on a wire while the couples of the crowd stopped along to chat, often to say how much they missed "good old Hank" or reminisce about "Dave's smiling face" at these gala events.

To the widows they usually said, "How are you getting along these days?" To which the widows answered, "Fine, thanks, but...." And that was that. Any single men at the party concentrated on the married women, for a number of reasons too exasperating to mention.

There is no reason on earth for me to expect my still-married friends to be more concerned or wiser about widows at parties than I have been. They'll find out soon enough for themselves. The same is probably true of your hostess days. We are not trained to be socially adept single women. That's a new skill for us to acquire; a challenge we must not ignore.

We can all see, when we are willing to admit it, we do not belong in the coupled world any longer. Not in the sense of husbands and wives in the social setting which conventionally centers around even numbers. Four in a car is fine. Five is uncomfortable in today's cramped back seats, and so forth. Aside from such complications, however, consider this: We widows remind men in their 60s of their own vulnerability, their own perishability. We are living messages to our women friends that they will almost certainly be in the same boat one of these days.

Some married women seem to think of any single woman at the party as a threat to their own marriages. That says something about their shaky marriages, but more about their self-esteem.

Being a widow is not the worst thing that can happen to a woman. Most men don't want to know that. Many of their wives just don't want to think about it at a dinner party or, worse still, a weekend in the country. Some married women have a tendency to glare at me across their buffet plate of Mexican chicken and tossed salad when I admit I have just returned from a trip to Paris for lunch (an exaggeration, of course) while they have been watching their husbands fly-fishing for the thirtieth summer in a row. Or they are still spending weekends watching good old Charlie sleep in front of TV after he finishes cleaning the garage on Saturday afternoon. Such thoughts fill these women with guilt feelings. Better they should get the message I should have heeded in my own marriage and say, "Charlie, the garage can wait. We're gonna go watch the whitewater races on the river this afternoon," or some such. Charlie deserves more credit than he gets sometimes. But for now, neither husbands nor wives relish the company of a freewheeling widow whose world is wide open and independent of men, chatting happily in front of their spouses. "Widows are such a bore. Why can't they just stay home like the rest of us?" some women will say, but the edge of envy in the voice is hard to disguise.

48

This brings up our obligaton as widows to be thoughtful guests. Here is my guest list of DO's:

Contribute to the conversation without dominating.

Be alert to opportunities to be helpful without being in the way or suggesting "better ways".

Check with your hostess about her well-laid plans before arriving at the front door laden with your marvelous homemade cheese puffs or YOUR favorite wine.

Talk sports with the men, diets with the women, and grandkids with everyone.

Offer on weekends to sit on the floor and play cards with small children, if necessary.

One DON'T is enough: Do not mope around or talk about the good old days unless someone else brings up the subject. Then smile a lot.

So who needs a ride to the party? You don't. Neither do I.

CHAPTER 10
New Contacts, New Skills

This is where the excitement really starts. Out there waiting for us is a wide world we have never explored. Oh, we might have been experienced travelers or not, we might have several college degrees or none, we might have had rewarding careers in our younger days or not, still, our world has more for us to *do* than we have imagined. Until now, we hadn't the time. There's one catch to taking advantage of the time and opportunities available now: We must get off the old duff and do it ourselves. No mother or teacher is going to spoon-feed us. This is self-help to the nth degree.

Every four years, the Junior League of Pueblo, Colorado, raises thousands of dollars with their Follies. In 1984 I was performing with my regular group, the Red Hot Mamas. For almost 30 years without a break I had been on stage in one act or another for the League, hamming it up and loving every minute. One unforgettable night of dress rehearsal in '84, the woman ahead of me in the make-up line turned to face me.

"I'm glad for a chance to talk to you. I've been wanting to thank you."

"Thank me?" I was mystified. Never saw this woman before in my life. "Whatever I've done, you're welcome."

She did not laugh. "Four months ago my husband died. I've had an awful time getting hold of myself. I've been sitting in the house all alone. Then I read the article in the paper about the Follies, saying the Junior League wanted townspeple to try out. And I remembered watching you in the last Follies when you were on that stage just weeks after your husband had died. At that time I thought, 'She's a gutsy lady.' So I came to try out even though I've never done anything like this before. I'm in the chorus line in three numbers having a good time, getting out with new people, learning to smile again. So thank you."

We hugged and I cried. She didn't.

How often does it happen, I wonder, that some small thing we do has a real effect--good or bad--on someone we never see? Singing and dancing did a lot for that woman's morale, her sense of her own worth. Even more important she was doing something she'd not tried before, really turning a corner in her life, making a real change. Her conversation with her fellow performers included plans for getting together after the Follies experience (I eavesdropped). She was out among'em again in a way that did not depend upon her husband. She was dropping the safety net, moving on her own steam.

My friend Jenny has been visiting back in Colorado. She lives in Atlanta now. Jenny has been divorced and has been slightly lost, you might say. During her stay in Beulah, we were fascinated because Jenny has been taking a course in magic at Emery University. "Have you always been interested in card tricks and stuff?!" we asked.

"Oh, heavens, no, I just saw the course mentioned in the paper and decided it would be fun, a way to meet interesting people, and something new for me to think about."

Jenny delighted and mystified us with her card tricks, and regaled us with accounts of the class taught by the chairman of IBM. The International Brotherhood of Magicians. Now we're all trying the tricks on our own families and friends. They think we've gone a little bonkers, but love us for it.

Jenny also told us of the great time she had as a volunteer clown in the Macy's Parade in Atlanta. In costume and clown makeup, Jenny and a woman who works with her marched all the way down Peachtree Street. Glorious. Now her old associates in Colorado are taking a second look at our own lives. Maybe the State Fair Parade or the Rodeo....

This is NETWORKING and it works. With our eyes and ears open, we can find new and marvelous things to do, then pass the magic along to other women like us. It works especially well in my life in the writing field, but we'll discuss those details in a later chapter.

For now, let's examine the ways we can all expand our circles of friends and our areas of interest:

1. Community colleges and state universities offer reduced tuition for seniors and special courses for "returning students." Included here are the Elderhostel programs. Any school or library can help you

with detailed information. Courses include those subjects you want to study for your own satisfaction (languages, anthropology), as well as practical stuff like computers.

2. Libraries all over the country are getting into the act with "writers in residence" and readings of local poets, etc. Also big in libraries these days are the film series, if you are more passive about knowledge but enjoy something more stimulating then re-runs of "Dallas."

3. Local art museums are running more and more excursions to nearby major galleries and exhibitions as well as sightseeing trips based on a common interest in architecture and art. Go along, by yourself the first time if you have to. There will be congenial fellow passengers looking for much the same lifestyle challenges which intrigue you. Being a docent is okay, of course, but traveling to other museums is more broadening.

4. Some concerts and theatre groups offer oldsters the joy of seeing many performances as ushers. This is true at SPAC in Saratoga Springs, with the San Francisco Opera (I understand), and other such quality places. A phone call to any such facility near you cannot cost anything and might open untold new doors in your life.

5. Certainly in every community there are senior centers where you can be entertained, enlightened, or be of service. Any local newspaper can fill in those details.

"But how do you start? I'd be terrified to walk into a college classroom at my age. Weren't you afraid you'd make a fool of yourself?" I hear a lot of this kind of talk, so I'll tell you about my first days in the classroom at Adirondack Community College. That fall semester I took Creative Writing, Basic Design, Poetry and (as I recall) Spanish I. Bear in mind that older students are not as rare as during our school days. I was not the only over-30 in any of these classes, but the majority of students were just out of high school.

In Creative Writing, I was looked upon as Teacher's Pet because Professor Rikhoff and I had been friends for a year or two before I decided to attend ACC. It took a while for my fellow writing students to accept me as one of the crowd, but it happened gradually. Outside the classroom is where much of Creative Writing pays off, with one-on-one discussions over coffee and such. Those kids didn't want to confide in some imported senior citizen who would go ratting off to the teacher about their problems with assignments. When they realized I had writing problems akin to theirs, the Big Thaw came.

Basic Design did not work out at all. I was the only student with bifocals. This made it impossible to focus on the papercutter. The nervous little beard-o who taught the course would instruct us to make all sorts of cut-out combinations of circles, rectangles, squares. Fine. Then we had to put our work up on the board. All of my rectangles listed to starboard. The squares were innocent of any right angles. The circles resembled hard-cooked eggs. My rubber cement seemed to smear more than that used by more accomplished students. I am a Design Drop-out.

Spanish class was fun. The professor expected a Coloradoan to have a working knowledge of Spanish, particularly a more-than-middle-age woman from a town with a name like Pueblo. The college bookstore had understocked on Spanish texts. I had to wait to buy my book. When Professor Spitzer called on me for a translation, I sat helplessly in the back of the room, blushing because my homework was not done.

"Porque, Senora Weaver?" ("Why?") He scared me.

"Porque," I stammered, trying to recall freshman Spanish from 1941, *"Porque no tengo...*book-o."

My classmates thought this was hilarious. We were all friends on the spot.

This is a good place to explain to you what kites have done in my life, particularly because anyone honestly wanting a new direction in life can find *something* of interest which might work miracles.

I did say "Kites." Kites have opened more doors for me, made more new friendships and started more juices flowing in my life than anyone would dream possible. In the first place, kites make friends. Kites become friends. To fly a kite is a challenge and a pleasure to be enjoyed alone or in a crowd. My kiteflying days began in 1974 and will not end until I am totally incapacitated.

Peggy Gandy introduced me to kites when I was 50 years old. She had discovered the Kite Revolution in California; the glorious new 25-foot dragons made of silver mylar, the German *Schmetterlings* and the Indian fighter kites. Peggy was a life-enhancer; what she enjoyed, she shared. Our first kitefly and picnic was an absolute revelation. Our kites (mine was borrowed from a nutty friend) soared, whirled, dipped and tangled over Ernamarie's pasture like nothing I had seen before. Four of us were hooked. We became the Beulah Valley Association for Tethered Flight. Three more members were added because they had fine pastures. And my life was changed out there on the Beulah Road, hanging onto a nylon line, thrilled by the antics of a weird-looking nylon half-mattress in the sky.

What if Peggy had said, "I never could get a kite up when I was a kid," and stuck to her knitting? What if my other friends of the B.V.A.T.F. had scoffed at the idea of women our age flying kites,

"That's the silliest thing I ever heard of. Me? Taking time out to have a picnic on a weekday, and try to fly a kite?" Worst of all, what if we had had an attack of the guilties and insisted on bringing the kids or the grandchildren along?

What if we had all said, "I'm too old for such nonsense"? Too old to spend time out in the fresh air with good friends challenging ourselves to acquire a new skill, find a different pleasure in our surroundings? Too old to study a bit about aerodynamics, nylon lines and flexible kites which had been invented long after our fumbling attempts at tethered flight with plain old diamond kites made of newspaper and balsa wood? Too old to do something new?

My first writing for publication was about kites. Before that article, the B.V.A.T.F. sponsored kiteflies and festivals occasionally, but like most kitefliers, we preferred making our own fun with kites as members of the Beulah Valley Association for Tethered Flight.

On cruise ships I have made new friends through kites. Every Christmas I am delighted with letters from the Binswangers of Philadelphia, the Merritts in Indianapolis, and the Kuhns in Ohio because we flew kites together from the afterdeck of the Royal Viking Star. My mail includes clippings about kites from all over the country. From as far away as New Zealand I have been sent kites as gifts. Little kids stop me on the street to talk about kites. Best of all, I have heard my grandchildren brag about my skill with a kite in their neighborhoods.

Around the world I collected kites which I exhibit in libraries and schools with great pleasure. In Glen Falls, New York, I am introduced as Fran Weaver, the Kite Lady. On any beach, in any mountain pasture, in any city park, I can be certain of bringing happiness to total strangers with a kite, all because of Peggy and her picnic.

Why tell you this? It can happen in your life, as much or as little as you want--whether you choose a craft, a collecting hobby, something more athletic or more artistic, whatever--your life can be the center of an ever-widening circle. "This is a time of final options," I quoted earlier in this book. Those options can be simple, and simply marvelous.

CHAPTER 11
Our Place or Mine?

"I've made up my mind. I'm going to stay in our big house one more year. That will make 25 years I've lived there. Then I'll move to someplace easier to take care of."

Joanne made this announcement at a dinner party last winter. Nobody had asked her about changing her living arrangements but the statement seemed necessary for her right then, in that crowd. We all knew Joanne had been debating the question of moving out of her house for several years since Bill had died and the kids had homes of their own. Any stranger hearing her incessant conversation about moving would have thought she was deciding to dismantle Mount Vernon or the Hearst Castle. Actually, she lives in a nice-enough four bedroom house with a big yard near the golf course. A salable property but no showplace. Around the room at this gathering, we all nodded politely and continued other conversation.

What I wanted to ask was simple, "THEN what will you do, Joanne? Talk about moving?"

Years ago, I decided that moving is a lot like making love:
1. You hope for satisfaction when it's over.
2. Experience is worth more than advice.
3. The less conversation, the better.

I still feel the same way about this question of changing homes, even as a widow. Particularly as a widow. We do hope for satisfaction from a move, but in different ways than during our mothering, married days. We used to need more bathrooms, larger closets, a family room for the kids and a separate bedroom for as many as possible. We used to covet big fenced yards for the toddlers to roam in or the dog to be safe. There used to be a hoop for basketball over the garage as soon as we moved in.

Now we can be satisfied with less space, but different priorities. An attached garage leading directly to the kitchen would be nice since we carry our own groceries. Fewer steps might be helpful since some of our friends (not us!) are getting along in years. Having less to dust and more freedom from household responsibilities are certainly on the plus side, especially if we have determined to get on with these last 20 years in a style befitting a woman of our intelligence and good sense.

Experience does count for a lot in moving, always. Good or bad, we have learned about houses, apartments and rental properties. We are able to evaluate our own needs. If experience tells us we need a larger place and a houseful of family "treasures", so be it. If experience tells us housekeeping is not as much fun as it used to be when the family came trooping in saying, "Gee, the house looks nice, Mom," before they messed it all up, then we need to find our fun elsewhere. Experience has taught us moving can be a headache, but it can be an improvement in our lifestyle and a boost to our egos. Few of us have chosen or furnished a nest of our own on our own. This is stimulating and frightening at the same time.

To hang pictures just where we want them, move them without someone yelling about "more holes in the wall," to shift two chairs and one couch a dozen different ways to suit only ourselves, to have pink or orange or puce on the bathroom walls if we like it, to use throw rugs in the bedroom or tape favorite snapshots to the back of the door in the hall; those are options when we have a place of our own, chosen just for us. If we stumble over the newly-moved chair on the way to the bathroom in the dark, we have only ourselves to blame. That's okay. It's a part of being on our own.

Now about number three, "less conversation the better." Do discuss your choices about moving only with those directly concerned: your children, the rest of your family, and certainly your financial advisor. Then keep your own counsel. As many opinions are available as you might want to find. What we all need in this time of our lives is confirmation, not well-meaning instruction. After too much carrying-on about whose sister was miserable/ecstatically happy in Scottsdale or Sun City, the fun of the decision is gone. The outcome is doomed. Trust yourself about making a move. You know enough to make up your own mind.

My primary reason for moving out of the family home when John died was basic: After the death of my father-in-law John and I went to Kansas to clear out his parents' house. His mother had died years earlier, but neither of those people had thrown out or disposed of *anything* in the 50 + years they lived in that one house on Republican Street in Concordia. Every room of that place was filled with strange collections of things--just things--and memorabilia which broke your heart and your back at the same time.

John had said many times to his father, "Don't you want to get rid of some of this, Joe? You don't need most of these things anymore."

Joe's laugh was unforgettable. "That's a lot of trouble for me, Johnny. I'll just leave that for you to do," like it was a good joke on his only remaining son.

Clearing out drawer after drawer, closet after closet, cupboard after cupboard of long-unused stuff, all of the good and bad times of John's life poured over him and there was nobody of his boyhood there to share the joy or the pain. Size five gypsy costumes for Hallowe'en, the layette of a baby brother who had died, broken Tonka Toy trucks and medals from long-forgotten track meets. Never had I seen anyone put through such an emotional wringer as my husband went through there. I finally called the thrift shop at the church and the junk hauler. We went home to Colorado, leaving all of those things. That's all they were: things.

I brought home one good keepsake from that lousy trip: determination that none of my offspring would ever have to go through such an ordeal because of me. Six months after their dad's death, I issued the summons: "Come and get whatever you want from this house. One week from Monday the Goodwill truck will take the rest." None of us has regretted that decision.

There are some women who seem to think moving from the home provided by their husbands is a sign of disloyalty or lack of appreciation. Some seem to hear a thundering voice from above: "You nagged for years for this house, now you act like you don't want it. Don't you understand how hard I worked so you could have two-and-a-half baths and a built-in dishwasher?" Times of our lives have changed, Ladies. You are on your own now. So am I.

What we are really facing is living alone.

CHAPTER 12
Me and My Shadow

Living alone means I can stay up as late as I want to or go to bed without waiting for the 10:00 o'clock news. Living alone means I can eat all of the Pepperidge Farm cookies without feeling I must hide the empty sack. Living alone means I can turn on as many lights as I want when I go to the bathroom in the middle of the night. Living alone means I can listen to talk radio to my heart's content. Living alone means I feel free to leave the mess of bill-paying out on the dining room table until I have time to finish the job. Living alone means I don't have to have a dog. Living alone means enough smoked oysters in one can. Living alone means staying late in town doesn't delay anyone else's dinner.

Living alone isn't a bunch of fun, but living alone is not all bad for a change. That's what it is for most of us: a change.

Like any change of the cast of characters in our little drama, this brings accommodation to new circumstances. For instance: Living alone means there's nobody to help carry in the groceries. Nobody to take out the trash. Nobody to laugh with over the Cosby Show. Nobody to play gin rummy or share scrapbooks on a rainy night. Nobody to say, "I love you."

I have learned to buy fewer groceries at one time, to use very small trash bags and make more trips to the bins outside, to ask a friend in for supper on good TV nights, to go to the foreign films or a lecture at an art museum when life alone is honestly a bore, to write lots of letters in the evenings, and to make my writing take up so much of my time and attention that I have little time to be bothered about being alone. Then I call someone to say, "I love you," and to hear that person say it to me.

During a writers' seminar on aging and women, the question was asked, "Why do so many women choose to live alone after 60?" Statistics were quoted; of women over 60, more than half of us are widows and 80 percent of us live alone. Very few older men live alone, maybe 12 percent. Aside from the expected, "I don't want to be a burden to anybody," the answer boiled down to one fact: widows in their 60s are generally truly single for the first time in their lives. One sweet-faced little lady in the seminar spoke up: "Listen. Until six years ago, I never had the bathroom or the refrigerator all to myself. I might save money by bunking in with somebody else, but as long as I can manage for myself, I'm not giving up my right to do exactly as I please around my own place." We all nodded approval. We can make what we want of every day on our own, and that's just fine.

The danger of living alone is boredom. Boredom is 99 percent self-inflicted; I've told you that before. So living alone brings the freedom but the responsibility for avoiding stagnation. We are self-propelled at this age. Unless we rev ourselves up regularly by getting out among'em with a real purpose in mind, we'll find ourselves more alone than we intended.

But getting home to peace and quiet certainly is nice.

CHAPTER 13
Just Ask Me to Dance--Please!

"It's not the empty nest that's driving me around the bend. It's the empty bed. I'm only 60 years old. I'm still a young woman as far as...." Believe it or not, I hear this and similar complaints often when I'm talking to women my age, particularly widows. One woman even said, "I thought I'd be glad to be rid of the sex part of my life, but I really miss it."

One of my favorite descriptions of my own age has been, "I'm so old I've never even seen a StayFree Maxi-Pad." That's always good for a laugh, but invariably some older woman brings up one of the indisputable facts we have to live with: Most men in their 50s or older prefer younger women. Why? We have our own teeth, our shapes are no worse than 50 + men, we appreciate warmth and affection more than we ever did when we were harried housewives chasing muddy children or trying to keep peace in the neighborhood. We certainly don't have to fret about waking the kids or having more *of* them anymore. So why do men always seem to prefer women in their 30s or 40s--or 20s, even?

And why do I find my teeth on edge and the hackles rising on the back of my neck when I'm walking down the street with a man my own age who not only pauses to openly admire some bra-less girl in her tight jeans and ridiculous spike heels, but has the temerity to remark about such beauty? That's the way men are.

As with many other phases of widowhood in this book, I have my own theory. What do you think of this?

Ask a little boy who's the prettiest woman he knows. He'll say, "Mommy," most of the time. Ask a young man the same question. He'll name the love of his life, his young bride. These prettiest women are in their 20s. They both take care of him, pamper him, ask him what he wants for breakfast and kiss him when he skins his knee. When his prettiest mother gets older, he is a teenager arguing with her about staying out late or having a couple of beers. When his prettiest wife gets older, he sees her as a nagging wife who argues with him about their teenagers and the car and has a fit when he has a couple of beers. Or suggests that he fix his own breakfast.

When this man we're talking about was a youngster, there was probably some shrewish old crow on his block who wore pink print zipper-front housedresses and bedroom slippers, had her hair on curlers or in a net, and yelled at him for riding his bike on her sidewalk or playing cops and robbers in her shrubbery. That is his immutable idea of an older woman, and men's impressions are not easily changed.

That's why men prefer young women. They always have. Simple, but I have yet to find anyone who can prove me wrong in this theory or even argue about it. The few men who appreciate older women are more flexible in their opinions or feel more secure with their own age. I happen to think they're a lot smarter. Another prejudiced personal opinion.

So what's a ladylike, well-brought-up woman in her 60s to do with this situation? We are not about to hang around singles bars or place personal ads in the local newspaper. Happily, there are more and more places to go dancing to music of the '40's, more centers where oldsters gather one at a time. Risk-takers can find some solutions in those situations. Others sit at home and moan, or refuse to admit the true nature of their frustration. "I wouldn't want a man around again except for--companionship," some old ladies will blush to tell you.

One other indisuptable fact is operable in this discussion: There aren't as many old men as there are old women, no matter how they feel about the aging ladies. No matter how many diets we suffer through or how many stress fractures we endure in aerobics dance classes in order to fit into girlish dresses and look cute in shorts; no matter how we might study up on the Denver Broncos or the New York Mets just to carry on a conversation with a man; finding an available man to talk to is next to impossible sometimes. Finding one who finds us physically desirable is a downright miracle.

This subject came up during a counseling session I had with a young psychologist during a stress-management clinic. In the first place, he seemed astonished when I was pretty blunt about such matters. He probably assumed I'd forgotten about all that--at my age. I explained that a man doesn't have to sign a pre-marital agreement just to hug me, or worry about paying my Supplemental Medicare insurance because we go together to a fine restaurant where I cannot go alone.

"Any man's future is a lot safer in a free-wheeling slightly more than casual relationship with a woman my age than getting involved with a sweet young thing who will saddle him with three half-grown kids and a mother-in-law his own age," I told him.

That poor red-faced young man looked as if he might cry. When I finally shut up, he said, "Don't you have any prospects?"

I laughed. "No, Sonny, I don't. That's one reason I keep myself so busy, so satisfied with the rest of my new life, so surprised about what I can accomplish on my own, that I have no time to lie around feeling unloved in that sense of the word."

The universality of the feelings of older women hit me hardest in a conversation with a 70-year-old man who lives with his wife in a Leisure World back east. I was working on a proposed novel about people in retirement communities at the time, and he agreed to be interviewed.

"You'll have to include the sex life," was his first remark, much to my surprise. "Not only the old men. Of course we're still interested. That's a big part of our lives now. But I feel sorry for the women because so many of them are alone. You ought to see them. The minute some old guy's wife dies, the casserole brigade begins. All they want is to feel wanted, loved, warm again. Seems like they all want one more orgasm," he said thoughtfully.

Writers of books about aging usually insist upon the continuation of sexual drive and satisfactions as long as we are in good health, but few have any concrete suggestions for fulfilling these desires. My new mentor, B.F. Skinner, approaches the subject warily: "It is too bad that affectionate relations between people of different ages are viewed uneasily. It is hard to see what is wrong with love between people of different ages, provided it is mutual." Then he changes the subject. That takes us right back to the first of this chapter; old men and young girls, or vice versa, though Skinner does not say so.

In absolutely practical approaches to the dilemma of enduring sexual desire in women past the age when they can logically expect another marriage or even a lover, I am reminded of the most successful gynecologist in Kansas City many years ago. Some of his clientele were patients who had depended on him for treatment and advice for years. This wonderfully understanding physician had special "examining rooms" in his office equipped with vibrators where older women came for 20-minute appointments for self-administered therapy. In a doctor's office that sort of thing was okay. At home, it was unthinkable. His patients adored him for his thoughtfulness.

Since beginning the final draft of this chapter, I have talked with three or four friends of my own age. The responses when I mentioned this chapter are worth recording here:

"Well, it's nice to spend the afternoon in bed when you both feel like it. Much less pressured than when we were younger. More concern for each other."

"Just tell your readers it's a lot better after 60 than it ever was before."

And, "What's your problem writing about sex? You forgot?"

CHAPTER 14
Wilt Thou Take This...?

Okay. Let's talk about remarriage. It surely works for a lot of people. I considered it once, myself, and my attitude now is slightly negative. However, like the Methodist ministers of my youth, I am "reminded of the words of that fine old song: 'I'll never say never again again.'" Marriage is a fine institution for folks who feel the need.

Feel the need I did, almost six years ago when I met a nice little man on a cruise of the Panama Canal. He was a widower, soft-spoken, amiable, loved my jokes. Our breakfasts together on board ship were a delight. We promised to see each other again. Just friends.

After I had visited him once at his house and he had stopped over in Colorado to spend a few days with me, we were more than friends. The contrast of our relationship with my 34-year marriage was startling and refreshing. We did not argue about anything, particularly my kids or my bank account. There were none of the old-marriage conflicts which I had despaired of so often with John. I thought marriage to this man would be one idyllic journey of serenity for both of us. He figured out what I had on my mind, and refused to consider marrying me. Thank God for that.

During the next year we did some traveling together, my writing started to flourish, and the difference in our ages really began to take its toll. He was older. As he became happier with the sedentary life of "comfy evenings at home" when I had driven 200 miles to spend a weekend, I realized I was right back at it: watching TV while the man in my life snored on the couch. An extended trip together put the end to the relationship. Any man who complains about my kite collecting and tries to tell me how to spend what's mine has lost the old ballgame. His constant bragging about the fact that he had never allowed anyone, even his wife, to drive his precious car was the final turnoff. Regrettably, by that time he had decided marriage was a good idea.

From that experience I can say without reservation, breaking up a relationship is no better or easier at 58 than it was in junior high school. The old hurts, the vulnerability are terrible. Lesson learned: tread carefully when a new more-than-friendship looms on the horizon, or just peeks at you across the dinner table some Saturday night.

On another cruise I met the unforgettable widower who made a lasting negative impression. He was preparing a questionnaire for all of the women desperately wanting to marry him. He considered himself such a great catch, he was being very careful to avoid gold-diggers or women who just wanted the prestige of a husband as handsome, wealthy and altogether wonderful as he knew he was. He would place a blind ad in selected newspapers (*The Wall Street Journal?*) and have his attorneys screen the applicants for the position of Mrs. Marvelous. He confided the first two questions:

1. How much money do you have?
2. Do you get seasick?

Imagine that! I have never heard what sort of response his ad elicited, but I hope he got a real dog. With bad breath.

There are possible areas of conflict which must be ironed-out the second time around, no doubt about that. Oldsters getting married will not have 15 or 20 years to work out the kinks in a household, they'd better know each other pretty well before they start shaking orange blossoms at each other.

Here are questions bound to come up in a second marriage which need to be faced squarely by both parties. These are based on my own observations and by reflections on those days when the best thing I could say about my husband was, "He married well."

1. What do you feed your dog?
2. Where does your dog sleep?
3. How often do you expect your children to visit?

4. Do you keep family pictures in the living room?
5. How do you feel about small overdrafts?
6. Are you picky about leftovers? Salads? Cheese?
7. What is your idea of a great vacation?
8. Is your mother still living? Near here?
9. Do your children expect you to babysit?
10. Can you repair leaky toilets or dripping faucets?
11. Will you dance? Play bridge? Take a walk?
12. Did your first wife bake bread? Make waffles?
13. Do you know how to load the dishwasher? Fold sheets?

That's a start. All of you can finish the rest of the list. As for me, at this moment I think I'll prepare a questionnaire for aspiring gigolos. Only a couple of questions would take care of that.

CHAPTER 15
Hearts: Young--Hair: Gray

Two little old ladies were pleased to be seated together on a plane bound for Florida. "Ah, I'm happy to see you going to Miami. Last year we didn't see you in Miami."

"Last year we didn't go to Miami."

"So where did you go?"

"To Majorca."

"Oh. So where's Majorca?"

"I don't know. We flew."

Stories of my travels around the world would fill a book more than twice the size of this one. I am an enthusiast, a nut about going places. I always have been. My husband was not fond of travel just to get away. He loved to work. We stayed closer to home than most of our friends. Together we never went to Europe or even to Mexico. My life in the past six years has been spent playing catch-up with all of the tripping I had not done earlier. That's all right. John would not have wanted to go "chasing from pillar to post." I can imagine his voice saying just those words when I am buying kites in Bangkok or basking on a Greek beach.

Travel was necessary as a drastic break in the familiar routines of home in order to establish a life of my own after John's death in 1980. During that first year of adjustment I settled for short excursions to visit old friends; then I took off, starting with a cruise through the Panama Canal.

I was on a bus bumping over a rough road under construction outside of Beijing last spring watching Chinese road-building crews working with shovels and buckets. My friend Mary and I had dabbled in international shopping in Hong Kong, had toured a Children's Palace in Shanghai, had stood in awe above the excavated terra cotta soldiers guarding the emperor Quin's tomb in Xian, had walked through the Forbidden City and the Summer Palace in Beijing. We had eaten

Chinese food we could never describe to the folks back home, including the web feet of ducks served to us at a state dinner in the Great Hall of the People. We had flown over mainland China in an old Russian prop-jet. We had walked on the Great Wall and posed for pictures beside lions guarding the Ming Tombs. We were pleasantly tired --returning to our cruise ship--when our charmer of a Chinese guide announced:

"This is a long ride..." She said "rong lide." "...so I entertain you. I sing now."

She beamed at us, held the microphone carefully in one hand, waved the other hand gracefully and began in the flute-like singing voice of the Oriental: "In a cavern/ in a canyon/ excavating for a mine/ lived a miner/ forty-niner/ and his daughter...." She sang at least four verses of "Clementine," with a smile, a tilt of her head, which entranced even the gripers on the bus.

Then she sang familiar songs from "Sound of Music," with the Chinese accent which reverses l's and r's in such a wonderful way. When she started on that old American favorite (in her opinion) "Led Liver Varrey" the applause was wild. We sang along. What a privilege and what a joy, I thought. Then she sang Chinese songs and we clapped even more.

Thousands of miles from home bouncing along on a bus, here I was watching the building of a real rapport with these people from whom we had been isolated for so many centuries. In some strange way I'll never look at my own world through the same eyes again.

Any travel experience can be an eye-opener. You should have seen me with my friend Professor Rikhoff on the beach in Rhodes. A couple of Gibson Girls in Gay Nineties bathing costumes would not have been any more conspicuous.

The sky was clear, the water an unbelievable sea green shading into deepest blue. Visible on the horizon was the mountainous coast of Turkey. In close-order rows along the beach were thousands of umbrellas and lounge chairs. And there we stood wearing our standard American one-piece swim suits--two middle-aged women on a topless beach.

My friend the professor and I were on Rhodes--a stunning semitropical Greek Island which is the Mediterranean mecca for northern Europeans, mostly sun-worshippers. All day long they lie there grilling themselves to a golden turn clad in nothing more than a G-string. We were overdressed, to say the least. We might just as well have been wearing one-piece black woolen Jantzens with red diving girls on the skirts.

Maybe we would have looked a little better without the shoes. Hot sands and rocky beaches of other islands prompted us to sport Chinese slippers--the ones that look like "Mary Janes." The professor had her Gertrude Ederle swim cap, which didn't do a lot for the image, either.

One glance up and down the beach made it chillingly clear. We had the only covered bosoms on the whole beach, a beach that stretched for at least two miles.

In forty years of practice, my gynecologist did not examine as many bare breasts as we saw on that beach in one hour. Those sauna-weary Scandinavians are the least self-conscious people I have ever seen.

My first feeling was outrage: Have they no shame? Then I tried to be cosmopolitan--cultural folkways are of interest to world travelers, I told myself. Then I remembered a class in comparative anatomy, but it was nothing like those girls parading on the sand. When I spotted women my age and older who had also shed their modesty, I gave up. Too bad they didn't.

There are many expressions about being in the minority. "Bastard at a family reunion," and such. We felt that much out of place among those nearly-naked beauties, but we persevered, determined to get a tan. That out-of-place feeling paled soon afterward when we found ourselves a part of the backpack set; and there is nothing like a night in a pension in Turkey to reinforce appreciation of the Good Life. My friend the professor and I learned that lesson the hard way--trying to be Mother Good Sport to a couple of backpackers.

"Now this is going to be fun. We can put up with anything for one night; and it's cute of these kids to invite us to team up with them --a real adventure." We kept telling each other such nonsense as our new friends led us to the rooms they had found in Marmaris, a miniscule seaport on the Aegean coast of Turkey. The bus to Ephesus was full, so we were spending the night.

Our first look at the chosen pension--double rooms with shower for three dollars--should have been enough; but the girl from Chicago had said, "There are a lot of steps," in a manner suggesting we oldsters might need assistance. That was a challenge not to be ignored.

The landlady was a delight, and beside herself with the prospect of four American guests. She ran ahead--up more steps--into Number Two, motioning the professor and me to follow. Number Two was a dingy green room with four cots, no rugs, three old bedspreads tacked up for curtains, a bare bulb hanging from exposed wiring in the middle of the ceiling, and a picture of Ataturk in one corner.

The professor stared at the four cots, then at the Danish boy who had become our fellow traveler. "Oh, no, Danny! Not four to a room!"

"Paula and I will be next door. Don't worry."

To find the shower, we were led through Number One back outside, down the steps, thence into a concrete cave equipped with a shower head suspended from the ceiling not two inches from another bare light bulb on an extension cord. Electrocution in a Turkish shower crossed my mind. The toilet was up on our floor past Number Three--the last room. It was that gem of modern Turkish plumbing: an indoor porcelain slit trench with a bucket.

It felt like camping, but we were tired enough to sleep.

I wakened, certain it was time to get up, and tiptoed to the bathroom to look at my watch. Ten minutes after twelve. I stole a sheet from Number One for a cover and went back to bed. In another two weeks it was four-thirty, and the professor said she'd dreamed she was digging a bed for herself in some dirt.

As if cots made of cardboard and sand, and chill breezes were not enough, there were the noises. One demented rooster crowed all night. Donkeys brayed. Dogs fought. There were bells and whistles and motorbikes. A constant drip filled the bucket by the toilet.

The next night we checked into the most expensive hotel in Kusadasi, Turkey--a medieval fortress of great beauty and charm and modern plumbing built to be a stop for caravans in the fifteenth century. No camel driver was ever happier to hit that place than we were.

CHAPTER 16
Get Set--GO!

Travel is not simply seeing new places, we've always known that. Now travel becomes even more important to us in widening our horizons at the time in our lives when time is what we have the most of.

There's no need to go all the way to China for a woman in her 60s to expand her horizons. Unless you live in the middle of Death Valley there is someplace interesting--even new--for you to explore within a day's drive of your home, perhaps half-a-day. Try this, for example: Spread a road map of your area on the table. Draw a circle with a 300-mile radius around your home with a jar lid or a small dish. Within that circle you'll find all sorts of out-of-the-way places to go and things to do. Second step in the process is to call a couple of friends and arrange a day trip or a two-day trip just for fun. Choose a new place or return to old haunts, but GO. That's a start toward weekends, group tours, travel clubs, cruises, specialized excursions, off-season bargains--even getting into the travel business yourself.

Before we go any further, lets' get one thing straight: traveling with other women is not the same as traveling with a man. We all know that, too. From luggage handling to dancing on cruise ships; from dining in fine restaurants to understanding the rate of exchange there's nothing like having a man at your side. We have to accept that fact and adjust our expectations, then we can have a good time. Women of our age are used to the protection of having a man around. We are not the most liberated or self-sufficient generation. We were not raised that way. We also appreciate the fact that men can be impatient shoppers, picky about the way their eggs are cooked, and absolutely impossible when it comes to asking directions after making a wrong turn.

It is not unusual these days for unmarried couples to travel together. That can work very well--to the advantage of both parties, as the saying goes. This is a new freedom for people our age, and more power to you if you can make it work for you. Here's an example of what can happen, however:

I was in New York with a bachelor friend whom I had known for years. We were going up in the elevator in a fine hotel. Two men were in the elevator with us.

"Oh, NUTS!" said I, "I left my purse on the floor beside my chair in the restaurant."

My companion smiled and pushed the button to stop the elevator at the next floor. "No trouble," said he, "We'll go right over and get it. It's okay. Don't worry." He patted my shoulder. The two men gave me a knowing stare.

Outside the elevator I turned to my old friend. "Now look here, if we're going to travel around looking like we're married, you'll have to shape up your act."

He seemed confused.

"In that elevator, you were supposed to yell at me and say things like, 'Can't you hang on to anything?' or 'This is the third time this week you've lost that blasted purse.'"

He understood; but I didn't lose my purse again.

A man who is not your husband might not enjoy hanging around while you choose gifts for eight grandchildren. That depends on how charming YOU are, I suppose, and how many grandchildren he has to shop for. Those are the choices we face in our new world.

I see nothing wrong in being a tourist or looking like one. Tourist attractions have that name because there is something there worth seeing or doing. Now that we do not have children in school or any other valid reason to take vacations only at the height of anyone's season, we can save money and stress by traveling after the crowd leaves or before they get there.

I act like an absolute tourist most of the time, except when it comes to the camera. Then I try to be nicer--not like those boorish fiends who take hours and hold up traffic trying to get a perfect shot of something already immortalized on ten thousand postcards. I take a lot of pictures in very little time--out of the windows of buses and standing on street corners, hoping for decent snapshots from at least one-third of the exposures. No sense in overloading my expectations.

Lately my photographic adventures have been fascinating: I double-exposed one-half of a film when I was in Oxford. This made for astonishing superimposition of statues on church steeples--a hit at any supper party. My other adventure with the camera was pure altruism. At the entrance to Mesa Verde National Monument, I spied a family of young Japanese. The father was taking a picture of the mother and two adorable round-faced children. I pulled my car to the shoulder of the road in a hurry and rushed up to the young man, offering in my best sign language to snap a picture of the family together. I can still hear myself:

"You stand with children? I take picture for you?"

I went into my imitation of a charades game waving my hands in his face, pretending to hold, aim, and operate the Nikon in his hand. He smiled gratefully and ran to stand beside his wife and kids. When I handed back the camera, he thanked me politely. He was a pediatrician from Seattle, or some such place.

When I got back in the car, my grandaughters said, "That was really nice of you to be so helpful to our foreign visitors, Oma."

I probably blushed. "They were Americans, Sarah, just like you and me. I hope I didn't insult them with my silly antics--I should have spoken English to them to find out who they were."

Back to the subject of off-season travel:

Airline rates are always lower, so are hotels. This is not to suggest spending time in Florida or Palm Springs in the middle of July, but early autumn is good weather almost anywhere. So is late spring. Sensible planning is part of the game, whether we go alone or with a group.

My friend Professor Rikhoff and I planned almost a year for our trip to Greece, Italy, and France in 1984. She planned much more than I did. Consequently she got much more from the two-month experience because she had crystalized her expectations. I learned a lot from that.

Travel magazines and the travel sections of the big newspapers are full of ads and information, specific and general, about any place we can think of and some we've never heard of. There are also tourist bureaus in New York and California representing almost any country in the world, particularly those with their own airlines. They are more than eager to send information to prospective tourists; so is the Travel and Tourism Bureau of every state in the union. The addresses of these bureaus can be found through libraries or your travel agent.

Then there are the travel guides, *Europe on Twenty Dollars a Day*, and all that. A travel guide is not unlike a book about raising your baby. Nobody should have more than one such book. The conflicting advice in two or more might ruin your trip. The professor and I must have had 50 pounds of travel guides which we dragged to Greece. Every time we decided to move from one island to another we consulted local pamphlets plus Frommer, Fodor, American Express, and the Harvard guide for the backpack set. We found the Class B hotels to be clean, adequate, and fairly well-located but universally without luggage handlers. The books had not told us that. I should have had a garage sale before we left Athens to go to the islands because I carried at least three times too much stuff. We also stumbled onto some dandy beach hotels not mentioned in any book and some great food at next-to-nothing prices just by wandering in on our own. Our expert advice about travel guides is: decide on one you trust and throw the others away.

One of our more memorable restaurant finds was a tavern sitting alone on a hill on the far side of Mykonos, our first Greek island. The manager/chef/owner/waiter gleefully escorted us to his kitchen. We were to point out the food we wanted. Wonderful. We chose a huge fish to be grilled.

The professor sign-languaged a request for a napkin by pointing to her lap. Our host brought an oversize apron, tied it around her, and presented us with a huge fish to deal with in any way we could. We laughed and made real sport of dissecting the fish. The Greeks dining there laughed too, and the food was great.

An American girl at a table in the corner admired our apparent ease of communication and shouted in pure anguish, "Now can one of you women explain to this man that we want three fried eggplant?" We could not.

We rented a car on Crete where we saw amazing sights like the Lassithi Plain where there had once been 10,000 windmills (and the door on our rented Fiat refused to close). On a public beach on Crete we were fascinated by an English woman who stomped onto the sand fully clothed—hat, skirt and blouse, stockings and heavy shoes. From a shopping bag she pulled a pup tent of pink toweling. She stuck her head, hat and all, through a drawstring hole in the pink tent, covering herself from head to toe. Then she went into some kind of a Houdini-like gyration which made the pink tent look like a gunnysack filled with live chickens. Dropping the portable pink cabana with one pull of the drawstring, she calmly walked off into the water wearing her swim suit, leaving us sitting there on the sand, speechless.

In Greece, Italy and France we drove a rented car which afforded us a great deal of freedom to explore wonderful art museums and archeological wonders without getting involved in organized tours which waste so much time. Being in a car was a challenge because roads were not marked at all well in Greece and my map-reading in Italy and France left a lot to be desired. It was fun, however, and served our purpose for this kind of a trip. We saved money by being able to shop around for hotel rooms and to carry food for lunch along the road. A word of caution about long hours and distances in a car with just two of you: that's a lot of togetherness. Beware of frazzled nerves and long silences. Those are facts of life to be reckoned with.

Travel by car is generally easier if there are more than two of you without crowding the car or the trunk space. A good system of rotation came out of a driving trip with two of my sisters. Each person drives 100 miles in a stretch. No more. Then, by the side of the road, everyone gets out and stretches, does a few knee-bends, and generally unwinds. The driver moves to the back seat, whoever has been riding front seat takes the wheel, the back seat person moves to the front. Duties were explicit. The driver does nothing but drive, no air conditioning or fiddling with the radio. That's the job of the front seat passenger who is also the navigator. The back seat person is the resting driver, also in charge of snacks. Carry along crossword puzzles or Trivial Pursuit cards for dull stretches of road. Miles fly by.

1. DON'T CARRY ANYTHING. An 88-year-old woman who rides the buses regularly mails her clothes to the friend she's visiting. That's right. Mails her clothes. Isn't that marvelous? She has no luggage to wrestle with or keep track of—or wait for when it doesn't show up. Only a small purse goes with her. This is my best tip.

2. PLAN CAREFULLY BUT NOT TOO MUCH. Just because you're going to Southern California, DON't try to see all of your cousins, old neighbors and childhood friends in four days while rushing through Sea World, Disneyland, and Universal Studios. Give yourself enough time, (what's the hurry to get back to an empty house?) or concentrate on one or two purposes of the trip. Don't gather everyone you want to see into one big group. That spells disaster—each wants to see you on your own.

3. SHORT EXCURSIONS CAN GET YOU IN THE MOOD for major-league travels. Most women fail to see the advantage of staying overnight on a jaunt to see a show or visit the museums in a nearby city. Take time. You have lots of that.

4. LEARN TO HANDLE MONEY LIKE MEN DO. This means, keep small bills and change in your pocket where it's easily available for taxis, tips, and such. On the street in New York City in broad daylight I saw a kid grab the wallet from a young woman's handbag and race off through the crowd. That's when I started wearing only clothes with pockets while in transit. Besides, nothing makes a woman look older or more helpless than groping around in a nine-pound purse/satchel for a quarter.

5. SUPPLY YOURSELF WITH THE RIGHT DENOMINATIONS OF MONEY. Stop showing up for lunch with nothing smaller than a 20-dollar bill. We women tend to be content with the money that falls into our hands by chance--what the teller gives us when we cash the check, or whatever comes in change at the sales counters. It's just as important to have small bills or coins as it is to carry your lipstick and pictures of the kids.

This is only the beginning, Girls. Whether you're going to take a powder to Boston for chowder or a kyack to Quincy or Nyack you'll learn more about this as you travel on your own.

CHAPTER 17
Of Slow Boats and Taking Notes

Other forms of travel? In my opinion a woman alone should try a cruise at least once. Settled on board, your clothes are in the closets and drawers and your transportation, hotel, meals and entertainment are all pre-arranged and pre-paid. No luggage to lug, no buses to board unless you opt for the shore excursions. I love cruise life. You meet basically nice people with whom you have something in common. I have friends all over the country whom I have met in the past five years on cruise ships. It's a camaraderie I've learned to appreciate.

It is not necessary to fly to the Orient or to Europe to go on a cruise. There are fine small cruise ships on Chesapeake Bay, on the St Lawrence Seaway, to Mexican ports, in the Inside Passage to Alaska, and of course there's the Delta Queen on the Mississippi. There are even three-day cruises from Albany, Buffalo or Syracuse on the New York State Canal System. (We used to say "barge', but have dropped the term after 160 years.) There are many other such cruises I have yet to try: those ferries around Vancouver, for example.

A woman need not be a millionaire to take a cruise but one rule of thumb is valuable if money is a problem; isn't it always? Look for the least expensive room on the most expensive ship going where you want to go. That is probably the most valuable, useful advice you will get from this book, so pay attention. Also: the longer the cruise, the older the crowd. Women our age tend to prefer the music and entertainment planned for the older crowd, but if you're looking for a younger man...

Whatever accommodations or age range you are seeking, take your request to an agent who will take time with you. Find out which of the many cruise ships she (or he) has sailed on, where the agent or others from the office have been. Ask about off-season rates and special promotions. The agent will appreciate your having a written list of questions when you call the office so that travel can be tailored to your tastes. Feel free to ask for brochures for comparison of stateroom size. Find out if there are two seatings for meals and avoid that if you can--it means an overcrowded ship. And do not be afraid to make a reservation, then change your mind. This is a big adventure and a big expenditure--get what you want from an agent you trust.

The most relaxed people I see while traveling are the folks who have simplified their lives while on the move. Even before I was single, I acted as a tour director for the Colonial Dames of Colorado. We went down the Mississippi and up to Alaska, as well as other trips. Since then I have conducted groups through the Panama Canal and in New England Fall Foliage. The travelers who have the least fun are the ones who carry the heaviest purses. God knows what those women have in those satchels, but they hang on for dear life and wear themselves out hoisting their purses onto the bus or into hotel rooms.

These are usually the same women who drag along big bargain bottles of shampoo, bulky hair dryers and six extra sweaters, plus shoes to match every outfit. I have shared rooms with traveling friends who could fill a bathroom counter, the dresser top and the desk of a hotel room with junk before I unzip my bag. All of this must be moved (often every day) and it weighs a ton. Just once, try a short haircut that can be toweled dry when you travel. It will grow out before anyone asks for your picture. Then bring along one good gray sweater that goes with everything. You'll love yourself for it.

As for those purses--I do wonder what's in them. Identification, a credit card or two, passport, travelers' checks plus a comb, a lipstick and some Kleenex should suffice. Just don't take more than you can carry, ever. We live in a world where "redcap" is a forgotten word and "bellhop" is an endangered species.

Simply getting away from home, a change of scenery, is sufficient reason to travel but an additional interest or purpose is a big plus in choosing a trip. Many women are prone to visit wherever their friends want to go, just to be with the group. They often wind up on a beach when they cannot stand sand between their toes or on an antiques tour not knowing Chippendale from Hepplewhite.

For a while I was on a kick of concentrating on the finest of restaurants and major art museums around the country. A friend and I focused on food and art in Italy, then on our Eastern Seaboard, then in the Far West--over a period of almost three years. We put the icing on the cake, literally, when we hopped over to Paris for lunch and wound up spending almost three weeks immersed in the food, sculpture, paintings and architecture of Paris, Brussels and Brugge in Belgium, plus time in Canterbury and Dover on the way to London. We did no shopping, theatre, or ancient ruins. Those I'll save for another time, but the food and art concentration makes good sense for me now, since my early education had been singularly lacking in art appreciation and my interest in food is overwhelming.

On the home side of the Atlantic, Richard and I have studied museums in Williamstown, Massachusetts, as well as Boston (not only the Musuem of Fine Arts but the Isabelle Gardner Collection and the Fogg and Busch-Reisinger at Harvard). Our restaurants were chosen from critics' columns, not guide books.

In Philadelphia, New York and Baltimore we did the same thing, including the Brandywine Museum of the Wyeths in Chadds Ford, Pennsylvania, and Winterthur in Delaware. On that trip we included the fabulous public markets in those cities and the Italian street market in Philadelphia. There's a lot more to see in this country than Mount Rushmore and the Statue of Liberty.

Our culinary and art tour moved on to New Orleans, L.A., and San Francisco. Basically, we had one basis of comparison for all of those cities, and I feel qualified to have an opinion now.

I did sort of the same thing on a world cruise in 1983 when I shopped only for kites in every port from Hong Kong to Capetown. It's an approach to traveling I heartily recommend. One of these days I'd like to focus on country inns and private art collections beginning in the Northeast.

One great way to tour for specific purpose is with a like-minded group from a museum, historical society, university, or associations like the Smithsonian. In this way you have the advantage of having details planned for you and you are assured of congenial company. Too many women have a tendency to shy away from day excursions of this sort. Give it a try. You might wind up finding someone who, like yourself, would rather travel on his/her own. At least you'll meet people who want to go someplace instead of sitting in front of the TV all day. Look closely at publications of the National Trust for Historic Preservation, the Oceanic Society, the Smithsonian and others. They might be headed in the direction you're considering.

For any travel, the most important equipment needed after a passport is a note pad. The smallest size spiral sketch pads serve the purpose very well because they have a heavy backing and are well bound. Only with on-the-spot notetaking is it possible to sort out one day or one city from another. The notes need not be full-fledged diaries or journal entries. A word or two will suffice. Recall from these notes is pleasant and amazingly accurate.

It's fun to remember asparagus served on a tilted plate in Bournemouth, trout with tomato butter at La Musardiere in the south of France, salmon with lemon on a bed of fresh spinach at Chez Camille in France; the shorthand jotted in among the notes about Cezanne's walk in Aix. There are also underlined reminders about zucchini rellenos in Taos, New Mexico, and a marvelous lunch at the Mocha Cafe in Denver. That could be useful some day--my travel notebook--to pass along information, if nothing else.

The best use of that notepad is compiling the scrapbook of each journey after you get home. This is also a way to get more than double your money's worth from any tripping by reliving every moment as you take collected notes, brochures, local folders, menus, train tickets, some postcards and your choicest snapshots to mishmash together in some semblance of order in one of those dimestore albums with the big sticky pages. On a long chest in my Beulah house I have lined up a dozen or more of these "Safari Scrapbooks" hoping someone will rave over them one of these days. Even if nobody ever opens the covers, I've had a fine time collecting, sorting, snickering, and recalling good and bad times on the road and on the high seas.

Not all well-laid plans work out every time. Be prepared. I figured that out about American Express when I landed in London for a short stay and my hotel reservation had been fouled up.

"Now look here, Frances," I told myself--after the frustrated desk clerk had explained he had no reservation, no room, and no prospect of one--"You have two days in London. You can spend one day going crazy trying to find a room or you can get out of town to see something else while waiting for your cut-rate travel agent's crossing on the QE2."

The girls at American Express were just like the commercials: "We certainly can help you locate a hotel at the seaside close to Southampton, where you will board the ship."

"Good show, Old Girl," I said under my breath. "London will still be here when you come again with more time to see the city, anyway." Instead of a setback, or a dismal time in a huge city, I did enjoy the seaside town of Bournemouth for a couple of easy days. After all, Paddington Bear prefers Bournemouth.

Incidentally, being a lone traveler in time of such small crisis is an advantage. Two or three of us would have stood around for hours saying, "Well, I don't care. What do YOU want to do?"

That English adventure brings us back to cruises, particularly the QE2. She's a famous ship, and many of her passengers rave about her, but I will choose a smaller, one-class vessel every time. In my opinion, you might as well ride across the ocean in a replica of downtown Dallas as pay such an extraordinary amount of money just to be able to tell your bridge group or the Friday night poker set about "The Queen."

So what other journeys await us? More. Many more.

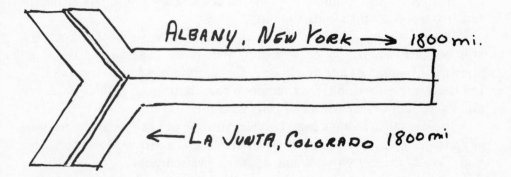

ALBANY, NEW YORK ⟶ 1800 mi.

← LA JUNTA, COLORADO 1800 mi

CHAPTER 18
Amtrak--The Road Back

Airports are terrible places, as far as I'm concerned. Granted, some are better than others, but any airport is basically overcrowded, too spread out, hard to park close to. The baggage seems to take forever to show up on the carousel, and people armed with backpacks and those folding little wheelie-things are constantly bumping into everybody. There is little that could be called peaceful or even pleasant about today's airports.

That's my principal reason for trying the trains. For several years I have been enchanted with the train along the Hudson from Albany/Rensselaer to New York City. The seats are comfortable. The passengers can walk around. The food is no worse than airlines, and you're not strapped in while you eat the stuff. I decided to try a long trip on Amtrak.

I boarded the train at bedtime one night in mid-December bound for Colorado and Christmas. The porter was helpful with the luggage. A cunning little basket of wine and cheese awaited my arrival. The bed was comfortable even though this was an old Pullman car--the kind where the toilet disappears when the berth is lowered at bedtime. Rhythm of the rails soothed my tired, fevered spirit and I wakened somewhere in Ohio for a pleasant breakfast and a relaxed view of the passing scene.

By noon we were in Chicago with a four-hour layover. The accommodating redcap showed me where luggage was checked and promised to meet me in time to help me board the train to Colorado. I could have gone to the Art Institute, but didn't realize I had that much time. The lounge for sleeper passengers was comfortable and quiet, anyway.

Out of Chicago my berth was in one of those glorious double deckers--an economy berth with plenty of elbow room and a huge window. Dinner was a fine roast chicken. The conductor announced bingo games and movies in the lounge cars. Before breakfast, Reuben the porter brought juice, coffee, and the day's newspaper for my morning pleasure. We smiled and chatted. The whole trip was just fine. I was in LaJunta, Colorado at 8:00 the next morning being met by son Matthew. No crowds, no fuss, no waiting for luggage that won't show up.

The trip took 36 hours. I did some writing, some reading, and a lot of sleeping. The compartment was almost a decompression chamber so I arrived ready for family and Christmas. The extra time was not wasted, it was my Christmas bonus to myself for the hard work I'd been doing--whatever that was. Now I'm writing to my congressman to beg him to keep Amtrak on the rails. For women like us, the train is perfect for travel and would be a downright party for two or three traveling together.

One word about those travel companions, please. Choose carefully. I mean, carefully. Some of the nicest friendships I have known have failed to withstand the rigors of traveling together. One reason is failure to spell out ground rules before leaving home; particularly about money. This might sound strange, but you'd be amazed at the way some of the "nicest" women we know can spoil a vacation by disagreeing about money. Some people prefer less expensive restaurants and Plain Jane hotels. Others consider the hotel and the food to be the major object of travel and want only the finest. Work that out before you even agree to go along, no matter how many years you and your proposed companion have played bridge every Monday at 1:30. She might be a real wildcat when it comes to splitting a dinner check. Beware.

How long can I be away? How far should I go? How can I be contacted in case of emergency? How many overdue bills will I be faced with if I stay away too long? These are important questions. Personally, I dislike being out of touch with my family for more than a week at a time, at least by phone, and I always seem to beat my postcards home no matter how long I stay.

Speaking of postcards, send some to yourself to add to your scrapbook, dated and with your comments for yourself.

One more travel tip, Ladies:

I could not believe a woman writer who visited me after a conference in Saratoga Springs. She prides herself on being a liberated, independent, feminist, activist woman-of-the-world. She had no idea how to go home to Washington.

This poor soul asked simple questions about buses, planes and trains as if she had been dropped suddenly on an alien planet. It is not always necessary to stick to a rigid schedule, but NEVER leave home without a fixed picture of the logical way to return to your home. This may sound ludicrous, but it does happen. Having round-trip plans could be called the prime requisite of successful travel for the single woman.

And speaking of returning home. Have you noticed how many friends say, "How was your trip?" and never wait for an answer? Don't be surprised. It happens all the time. One solution for that problem is a travel club--just a little one. I know of groups of women who gather for lunch once a month just to talk about trips. They exchange observations and travel tips, and sometimes plan jaunts together. This often gets some of the shy ones out of the house and away from "Edge of Night" or "Days of Our Lives" for a while. If you don't have a travel club or know of one, suggest to your agent that a travel club for older women would be a great service from her agency. She might let you be the president, or offer you a job.

Some travel agents welcome part-time tour directors who can get along with a crowd and plan excursions. We all learned a lot about that being den mothers, now we can put the experience to our own use. The normal arrangement is to work outside the office on a commission basis. Promotion of tours is the responsibility of the tour person, not the agency. This can fill time and bring in a little money, as well as affording the opportunity to travel yourself. After the first year, outside salesmen for travel agencies are entitled to agents' rates for personal travel. That's the best part.

My first trip to China was an agents' familiarization trip with my boss, Judy Smith. Later that same year we went to Sweden and the Scandinavian Waterways. I have sailed with Royal Viking both ways: as an agent escorting a group of passengers, and as a private passenger. Either way is fine with me. Rates at hotels and resorts are lower for agents. You might have gasped when I mentioned keeping two grandsons at the Waldorf Astoria. Agents' rates, Ladies. You can do it, too.

This tour business might be frustrating in the beginning but it can be rewarding. You'll find yourself providing opportunities for women who are fearful of venturing forth on their own. When it comes to getting on the road, being an employee of an agency is worth the trouble.

No matter how you do it, just get out there and GO.

Have a good trip!

CHAPTER 19
Join the Crowd!

In the process of writing this book, I have used many words, some of them too many times. But not once have I used the word, "Happy." Happy is not the point. Happy is the by-product of what we are discussing here. Quality of life is the business at hand. If yours brings happiness, that's fine. Sam Levenson said, "God never promised Mamma happy," in his book, *In One Era and Out the Other*. I tend to agree. Happy comes from our own efforts.

Where do we look for improvement in the quality of our lives? First of all within ourselves. We sit quietly with a pen and paper one day and make lists of "I can" and "I know" and "I have." Then we analyze the world in which we live. What are the other kids on the block who are your age doing these days? Where do they go? Does something in particular seem to work for the other older women in your church circle or in your line at the market? What's going on in town at your library or arts center? Or the YMCA?

We shy away from the term "support group" because that sounds like some outfit for sickies. Widows are not sick, we just need a sense of direction, a way to get rolling again in this new phase of our lives. Group counseling for grief therapy is readily available everywhere. Ask your doctor about that--or consult your daily newspaper. But for escaping from the humdrum ruts which seem to threaten us, help is accessible around every corner.

So far in the research for this book, and for the enhancement of my own life, I have sampled senior activities from lunch at SRDA in Pueblo, Colorado, to AARP in Hudson Falls, New York. In each instance, I was delighted to find men and women with vigor, enthusiasm, and a zest for living. In Hudson Falls there are 400 members of AARP. Now, Hudson Falls is just as small a town as its name implies. But the *waiting list* for AARP is up to 50. Meeting spaces can't hold the whole crowd. These people are busy planning trips to Nashville and other spots, contributing to community projects, and keeping up with legislation which affects oldsters.

At lunch in Pueblo, there was live music provided by a dandy ragtime piano and banjo. The food was fine. The crowd friendly and lively.

Don't be a snob about these places, Ladies. Don't decide you're not old enough to need a new friend or two. Don't let the idea of being surrounded by our peer group once in a while shut you out of some good times. I know many women who refuse to ask for a senior citizen's ticket at the movies or senior discount because of pride. That's foolish. Everyone is getting older. You're just ahead of the pack right now. Nothing to hide about that. Let yourself take part in activities geared to our age at least once. Surprise yourself by finding kindred souls who are coping with the same mishmash facing you. Find out how others manage. That makes any group a support group.

The woman most adrift when she becomes a widow is the woman who is unprepared, even in her own head. She is probably the person who has said, "If I die." Generally the same type who has always been surprised by Christmas coming so soon. This lady is the weeper in the supermarket, convinced she is the only wife in the world whose husband was "taken from her." She's a special case, not to be dealt with here. We're talking about sensible people who have at least thought about facing the inevitable.

Back to support groups: yours might be your bridge club if you work it right. That is, be open and honest about your feelings with close friends without monopolizing table conversation or haranguing the still-married players with your problems. My daughter plays bridge with seven women much older than she is. They keep track of each other. Understand each other. Now that it's more difficult for them to drive to take care of their own needs, the others are aware and helpful without trying to be nosey or dictatorial. But as chronic disease and really old age catches them, they need each other more.

Other "old crowds" are not as helpful, especially couples. One of the most miserable widows I have ever seen is a 50ish gal who expected to be included in everything the old gang did after she was alone. This sort of dependence is embarrassing for the old friends who are uncomfortable coping with an extra woman all the time. Five people in one car, for example. Do not treat your old married friends as a support group. They'll try hard for a while, Ladies, but many a long-lasting relationship has been wiped out by a third/fifth party always hanging around.

Farther afield are better support groups, even though we might not give them such a name. The local museum sponsors trips to bigger or other exhibitions. Most of the patrons are old ladies--just like you.

The library has programs of foreign films or readings by local poets and writers. Smart older women intent upon keeping their curiosities alive are to be found there. Your schools might need someone to help the children who cannot read. Other older people are doing that, too.

Best of all, your community college is a gathering place for older people who recognize the advantages of learning more for our own satisfaction. State universities have programs FREE to senior citizens who want to audit courses. No need to study for a degree. You're learning to please yourself. Yesterday I saw my Spanish professor from Adirondack Community College and thanked him for such a good time in his class. I could not say even that in Spanish, of course, but he seemed gratified by my greeting anyway. Fellow students from that Spanish class have become fast friends. We do other things together now. The same holds true for classmates from anthropology and creative writing. We get together. Keep track of each other.

Travel, carefully chosen, can provide moral support. Institutions like the Smithsonian attract participants in their travel groups who are generally older, often women. This is learning, traveling and making new friends all at once. Try signing on alone. You'll meet more people that way and the extra single charge is worth it. Two women side-by-side all the time on a cruise or other trips tend to be left to their own devices. On board ship or on buses you can strike up friendships with any number of women who are facing the same choices, the same headaches, the same opportunities you are. Some will become real friends. Others will be fine examples of what you don't want to be.

Now we come to the exciting part: Elderhostel.

Why I am just learning about Elderhostel I cannot say. I'm ashamed to admit I have not been paying enough attention. With this wonderful outfit, anyone over 60 can attend one-week courses on college campuses and other institutions of learning in every state of the union or study abroad. This is described as a program for older adults who want to expand their horizons and develop new interests. This is a support group of the highest order because it moves forward--takes advantage of the world around us. My own experience with Elderhostel is described in detail in the Addendum of this book. This just might be the cup of tea for you, too.

From Modern Philosophy at the University of Maryland to the New England Experience 1790-1840 at Old Sturbridge Village in Massachusetts, from Deaf History at Gallaudet University to American Indian writers of the Southwest at the College of Santa Fe; courses in nutrition, music appreciation, space technology, computers, theater arts, geology, cross-country skiing, ceramics and the

Oriental mind are offered at an all-inclusive on-campus cost of $205 per week. I can't stay home for that.

Elderhostelers live in country houses in Britain, study the flora and fauna of Bermuda. In Scandinavia, three-week programs may be spent in one country or divided into three. All over the world, including China, 60plus traveler/students are expanding horizons. These excursions include air fare, lodging, meals, even limited insurance at a fraction of the cost of individual travel.

And you can't find anything to do? Come on now. This is a support group *par excellence*. I'll even give you the address: 80 Boylston Street, Boston, Mass. 02116.

CHAPTER 20
Twenty Percent Still to Go

"All the world's a stage, and you are not the first to play the part of Old Person. The audience has seen the play thousands of times and knows your lines better than you do. The role you are expected to play is not flattering. The Old Persons who have walked the boards before you have been crochety, stingy, boastful, boring, demanding, and arrogant. They have complained of their illnesses and many other things. You may be surprised at how easy it is to play the part that way. The audience expects such a performance...."

Wonderful paragraph, isn't it? That's from *Enjoy Old Age* by Skinner and Vaughan, and it carries their book or this one in a nutshell. Just who are you going to be for the last act, the last 20 percent of your life? How much will the rest of your life characterize your feeling for life itself? Albert Schweitzer often referred to a reverence for life. We need to pay attention there. Old people tend to give the impression they're just serving out their sentence, and you'd jolly well better stay out of the way or wait on them hand and foot because they have put in so much time already.

"If you would play the role of Old Person in modern dress, you must learn new lines and new stage business." Skinner and Vaughan again. This means biting the tongue when tempted to extol the wonders of the good old days. It means shared interests with family and friends which might take an entire new direction from anything before in our lives. "The minor pain of arthritis" should be our secret, no matter how much it hurts. Other frailties and illnesses should be discussed only with someone who can *do* something about the problems. Not the girl at the checkout stand or your friendly bank teller.

One more quote from *Enjoy Old Age* fits here: "When played with skill the part of Old Person is marked by tranquility, wisdom, freedom, dignity, and a sense of humor." Also essential for the women of greatest interest to me--the women *like* me--is willingness to trust our own decisions. We all know more than we think we do. Decision-making is a trial to everyone. Experts quote statistics on influences from education to birth order in explaining the difficulties some folks have making up their minds. Let's add "self-confidence" to the above list of adjectives and find out how much more smoothly our lives run; how much more we accomplish without crying to the kids or the young man in the trust department for help.

The thoughts and suggestions offered here are based on good health. Here again, we must assume responsibility for ourselves. Even though walking half-an-hour or more every day seems stupid sometimes, even though our friends smirk when we mention doing aerobics in front of the TV or (better still) in a regular class, even though we really would like more salt, more eggs, more sugar, more butter, more coffee, more Milky Ways; even though maintaining basic fitness is a nuisance, the whole ordeal is worth the trouble.

Why? Simple. You or I cannot be all of those good things listed by the behaviorists if we don't *feel* good. If we haven't the energy to get on a bus and go with the group from the Hyde Collection down to the Met to see the Rodin Exhibition or a special show of the Impressionists, then how can we be the Fascinating Oldsters we want to be?

Same is true with your teeth, although my dentist will be astonished to learn I really care. Unless we have a mad desire to spend the next few years battling with dentures, Poligrip and glasses of blue stuff to soak our teeth in, we had better invest in the Waterpik, the floss, and the regular checkups, just like the kids. The least tasteful subject of conversation is false teeth. We can do something about that ourselves.

When we were girls we looked different, we dressed differently, we had aspirations and intentions almost unrecognizable these days. When we were girls the movies were censored, the music was hummable, the lyrics were memorable, the speed limit was 60 or 70, Little Orphan Annie and Ovaltine Shake-up Mugs were the biggest thing since sliced bread. We doted on "One Man's Family" and cried about Will Rogers and Wiley Post, or King Edward and Wally. We wanted to dance like Shirley Temple, sing like Judy Garland.

When we were teenagers we knew how many ration stamps were necessary for a bottle of catsup, if you could find any. We agonized over the newsreel pictures of the War in the Pacific or the Battle of the Bulge. We sang "Serenade in Blue" and "Deep Purple."

After the war, our skirt lengths went from the Dior New Look in the 50s to near-minis as we became new mothers; young matrons. We read Dr. Spock and endured Howdy Doody. Bantam League Football and Junior League were the order of the day. As volunteers, we contributed to the world around us. Inside the family, we encouraged straight A's and the budding careers of our workaholic husbands.

Now here we are, you and I, ready to take on one more slice of life. But we are still girls. Deep inside us, warm and cherished, is the same person who has done the best she could through whatever came into her life so far. The face is changed. But the Girl is here: the Girl with the Grandmother Face, and the whole world is gonna be glad we're still around.

ADDENDUM
Back in the Classroom
Elderhostel and Writing Courses

"Who ever thought we'd find ourselves back in the classroom— and loving every minute of it!"

That's the quote on the cover of the latest catalog from Elderhostel. In the Adirondacks I have affected a turn-around in my own life by attending Adirondack Community College. Now I find out I can keep the process going in any state in the union or almost any country abroad. I am just learning about Elderhostel. What I know so far is worth sharing.

Elderhostel welcomes anyone 60 or older to attend one-week courses in colleges and other institutions of learning across the country. This has been going on for years. It's a BIG program. I'm just catching up in finding out about it for myself.

For $205 per week including room and board, you or I can study Greek Mythology at Mississippi State, Architecture of Cape Breton in Nova Scotia, The Pleasure of Poetry at the Potsdam campus of the State University of New York (SUNY), or American Indian Writers of the Southwest at the College of Santa Fe in New Mexico. Languages, cooking, computers, archeology, religion and crafts are included in the myriad of offerings for the same fee. And each $205 entitles the student to three courses, not just one. Of course dormitories are not like the Ritz, and cafeteria food is not like dining at the River Cafe, but the groups are like-minded people of our own age which sounds like congeniality plus to me.

Some oldsters I know attend regularly. Orel and Blossom Friedman even went to New Zealand with Elderhostel for three weeks and had a marvelous trip. One man in Glens Falls has taken about 20 sessions on various campuses and swears each was worthwhile. Friends who haven't done Elderhostel seem to have cousins or sisters who've "been there."

The best way to enjoy the freedom and independence of these older years is to keep our heads working, our imagination and curiosity alive. When we can start a new conversation with our grandchildren, when we have a different subject to bring up at the bridge table or out to lunch with the girls, when we understand more of the world around us--in other words, when our awareness is working--we are more interesting to our family and to ourselves. That is one of the keys to successful aging.

Sitting back and saying, "I don't want to know...." or "I cannot remember anymore so I..." is writing our own sentence for really declining years.

This is my impression of Elderhostel after a week at the College of Santa Fe:

"We're all in our places
"With bright shining faces...."

There we were, all seated at our desks, coats piled on a chair in the back of the room, notebooks and ballpoints at the ready. Back in the classroom. And the faces were bright and shining--all 28 of us.

"Is this your first Elderhostel experience?" this tall, Ivy League-looking man with a well-trimmed beard and a well-dressed wife said to me.

"Yes. I'm really looking forward to this week," I replied, thinking I should have worn a freshman beanie or some such identification. "I've certainly heard a lot about Elderhostel. Have you been here before?"

"Not here," said the man. "But Barbara and I have attended other sessions in the Smoky Mountains, in Ireland, in Wales, on the East Coast. This must be about our seventh, I'd say."

"This is our fifteenth," the woman across the aisle chimed in. "Last one was to New Zealand. But we've been all over the United States. You should try the one on the Chesapeake Bay--or Alaska."

"This is my first." This from a little lady on my left. "I was spending the holidays in Albuquerque with my son and his family and wanted to know more about this part of the country. I live at Leisure World in Silver Spring, Maryland, and it seemed silly to turn right around and go home after New Year's, but my children are busy, so I decided to try this."

Of course I told her about my friends Grace and Ed at Leisure World, and we talked a little more about being the freshmen in the crowd. But we talked. That's the big thing. These folks are vigorous, eager, expansive, easy-to-meet, interesting people from all over the country. They came from Illinois, Florida, Connecticut, Ohio, Minnesota and so on.

And they are retired. The men are retired military or professors or businessmen. Some of the wives had had careers of their own. Some travel all winter to various Elderhostels, others would be going straight home. Each one, without exception, had something valuable to add to any conversation. Each of these people were ready for the challenge and opportunity of a new course in a different college, with more to absorb about the area, the Indians, the Southwest culture.

Our class sessions were stimulating. I had a hard time keeping up with my note-taking because I wanted to record the remarks, questions and comments of my classmates as much as the lecture. Elderhostelers are good listeners, good learners, and a fine bunch for hanging around.

"Well, what happened at this college course of yours? Did you stay out too late and get locked out of the dorm? Did they have bed check every night at eleven? Was there a room inspection to be sure you hung up your pajamas? Did you eat macaroni and cheese for a week? Any Spam?"

Those are questions from the cynics of my world who cannot believe this enthusiasm for a return to campus life, even for a week or two. I'll admit we do get pretty set in our ways--spoiled, perhaps--by having our houses to ourselves at this stage of our lives. A dormitory is surely a change.

I've tried dormitory life in several settings, ranging from Skidmore to Oxford to the College of Santa Fe, in the past few years. Go for it. That's all I can say. College people and college programs are great for us oldsters. The cost is reasonable, the food acceptable, and the rewards are enormous.

At the College of Santa Fe there are Elderhostel groups in the dorm 48 weeks of the year. The college is geared for our set. "We appreciate these students," we were told. "You don't leave graffiti on the walls or play ear-splitting music 'til all hours of the night. You're more gentle with the Coke machines. You are responsive and eager in the classroom."

The young woman in charge of the program in Santa Fe is pleasant but not condescending. She answers questions, hands out maps and shopping advice, arranges a tour of the city, and suggests opportunities for observing "local color." But she did not herd us around like mindless inmates. We saw the Museum of International Folk Art in one big group, but we visited nearby pueblos and weavers in a caravan we organized on our own. Some of the class saw "The Taming of the Shrew" performed by the local repertory theatre, with mixed reviews. Others of us watched Spanish gypsy dances and poetry in a wing of the Museum of Fine Art which seems to be an ancient church.

We all looked for Indians selling pottery and sampled New Mexican food on our own. In other words, these continuing education planners leave time for enjoying surroundings as much as classroom experience.

"So what did you study, exactly?" Another common question.

Traditions in Conflict

Mythology and Science Fiction

Literature of the Southwest

Those were the courses offered at the College of Santa Fe to the Elderhostel class of January 4-10, 1987. These are not the only courses ever offered there, but I felt lucky to have arrived for this curriculum. We had evening discussions of fiber arts, Indian traditions, and so forth, but in the classroom, this was it.

The first course, taught by a Christian Brother, concerned the roots of the Western Tradition and made me realize how little I had retained from M & M History 40 years ago. We thought through early exploration and settlement of the New World, the Industrial Revolution, and the rise of Marxism as well as various and sundry wars along the way, but the point of the course was the total effect of these events on our lives today. Somehow such considerations make a lot more sense now than in my freshman days at Colorado College. And the answers to "Where do we go from here?" are a lot tougher than before World War II. We talked, listened, and learned and some of the students argued with the professor, but not me. Brother Gregory teaches many Elderhostel classes and has his subject matter carefully organized for a five-day course. I wanted to hear what he had to teach us in his carefully prepared lectures too much to argue fine points about religion and all that.

What does Ulysses have to do with Buck Rogers or Darth Vader? That's what we discussed in our second course, Mythology and Science Fiction. Most of us admitted we care little for the science fiction popular today, but we didn't want to be old fogey enough not to try to understand. Each civilization has similar myths of truth-seekers, floods, exile, and such but it had never occurred to me that Isaac Asimov and Ray Bradbury were writing updated versions of the same tales. Now I want to read more science fiction. It really isn't as much trash as I had thought it was. Not all of it, anyway.

The third course introduced most of us to names like Scott Momaday--an American Indian writer who won the Pulitzer Price and made "Native American" writing respectable. This opened doors for many of my classmates about the beliefs, rituals, and customs of the Indians of the Southwest today.

Elderhostel is not the only organization offering continuing education for oldsters around the country. At Adirondack Community College, at Skidmore, at SUNY, all over the Northeast there are affordable college courses for any of us who want to be sure our heads work as long as the rest of our bodies. In the West it's the same. At Pueblo Community College, at the Arts Centers and the libraries, everywhere we turn, there's an opportunity to improve the quality of our lives by doing something different, learning something new. Let's try as many as possible. Nobody can know too much or have too many friends.

Maybe that's why Elderhostel had grown so rapidly from a single New England campus ten years ago to a world-wide network of colleges and other learning centers in all 50 states and most foreign countries. There are more old folks every day, getting older every day, and we need something to do--something to think about besides Medicare and fretting about what our kids are doing on Sunday afternoons when we are at home alone.

We had graduation ceremonies on Friday night in Santa Fe. Nobody played a flute solo or offered words of advice to the departing scholars, but one of our new buddies conducted an excellent quiz contest, and the evening ended with a joke-swapping session appropriate for any dormitory crowd.

Next I think I'll try SUNY/Potsdam for Spring Flora of the Adirondacks and then maybe an English Country House, and then....

Now About Writing....

"Starting to Write After Forty" is the title of the workshops I have conducted in the past three or four years. I'm not much of an expert about writing, but I am fully qualified as far as the age requirement is concerned. Constantly I hear from women who are fascinated by writing. They ask, "How can I get started?" "Who helped you?" "Should I have an agent?" "Where do you get your ideas?" and other such questions. I have now considered these basics enough to distill the answers:

Remember, these are only opinions based on my experience.

1. Talk to anyone you know who writes--for anything.

2. Check with your local librarian for information about writers' groups and workshops in your area.

3. Contact the community college or state university in your town--don't overlook private colleges, either--for writers' courses, particularly creative writing.

4. Write. Start a journal and add to it every day. This is not a diary. The journal is what you think, how you feel about any subject in order to explore your own feelings and your own facility for putting yourself on paper.

5. Read magazines like Writer's Digest or The Writer for advice about markets and methods of reaching publishers. There are excellent workshops all over the country where recognized writers in their fields take time to share knowledge and teach skills to aspiring authors.

6. Try all kinds of writing. John Updike says one essential for creativity is discovering your own genre. Are you a poet? a novelist? a nonfiction columnist? an essayist? a writer of short stories? a research expert? You'll never be certain 'til you've given yourself a shot at each sort of self-expression.

7. Form a connection with some sort of a group of your choice. Since my own experience is my greatest resource for discussing this subject, and since I started writing absolutely on my own except for one faithful friend who filled in the blanks for me along the way, I can only tell you what works for me. The Santa Barbara Writers Conference was my first connection with other professionals in a group. This has proven to be such a useful week of education and inspiration, I have returned to Santa Barbara every June since 1978.

My other alliance with writers is different: The 10-year-old International Women's Writing Guild is open to all women connected to/by the written word. These are not necessarily published authors who attend the workshops. The newsletter reaches more than 3,000 women across the country with news of local workshops, writing opportunities, and the work of individuals wanting to contact others interested in the same subjects. IWWG has an annual conference/ retreat at Skidmore College in Saratoga Springs, New York, and can be contacted through Caller Box 810, Gracie Station, NYC 10028.

8. Learn all you can about small presses and smaller magazines. The market is there for magazine free-lancing. Thousands of magazines are published which you and I have never heard of. *Writer's Market* lists these according to topics of interest and fills in details about how to submit, what you might be paid, and all that. The market for nonfiction is much larger than fiction in periodicals. Poetry is very hard to peddle, worse to make any money off of.

9. If you are really a neophyte writer, forget about finding an agent right away. Agenting is a complex, highly structured business. No agents take on magazine submissions as a general rule. The best way I can suggest is just keep going to workshops, conferences, to hone your writing skills and make connections. Then one day you will meet an agent interested in your work.

10. Finding a publisher is almost worse than establishing yourself with an agent, since the two are interdependent. Like that old song about Love and Marriage, you can't have one without the other. No writer/columnist/housewife in Colorado can sit here and give you the exact formula for succeeding with a career in writing--or an avocation. But I can tell you this: If you work hard enough and long enough, and are willing to accept some rejections along the way, you will find nothing in life more satisfying than seeing your own words in print, or being stopped in the supermarket or the lobby of the bank by someone who says, "I just want you to know I like what you write." It's worth the trouble, believe me.

Look for other inspired books by Frances Weaver

Midlife Musings

As Far As I Can See. . .

Distributed by

PRICE STERN SLOAN
Los Angeles

Frances Weaver is a freelance columnist whose writing career began in her 50s with the publication of an article about flying kites. Long interested in the opportunities and options open to women in their after-middle years, Frances Weaver has chosen to pursue writing as a means of exploring and sharing those possibilities with women concerned about the quality of their lives.

A Westerner by background and education, she now divides her time between residences in Pueblo, Colorado, and Lake George, New York. Her weekly column, Midlife Musings, appears in the Saratogian, Saratoga Springs, New York, and the Chieftain, Pueblo, Colorado. Her first collection of these columns, *Midlife Musings*, has been published in book form and as a book-on-tape in the past year.

Frances Weaver is a widow with four grown children and eight grandchildren. After the death of her husband in 1980, Mrs. Weaver chose a return to college as the vehicle for changing her lifestyle, living as a single for the first time in her life. She enrolled in Adirondack Community College in Glens Falls, New York, participated in workshop/conferences of the International Women's Writing Guild at Skidmore College in Saratoga Springs and developed the skills necessary for her chosen field of non-fiction writing.

In addition to keeping up with the demands of regular column production and promotion of her self-published books, Frances Weaver is a genuinely funny lady and a busy speaker, addressing civic groups and literary audiences in New York and Colorado.

Have you read Frances Weaver's other delightful books?
   Midlife Musings
   Speaking of the Girls
   . . . .books laced with wit and wisdom!

"Fran has a delightful sense of humor and it shows in her writings. In addition the hints she has for women in their sixties are not only wise but presented in a unique way which capture the readers attention."
                                                              R.H. Rawlings, Publisher
                                                              The Pueblo Chieftan
                                                              Pubelo, Colorado